Your Child Has Autism. Now What?

A collaborative guide for parents of a newly-diagnosed child

Casi Olson, M.A. in Clinical Psychology, LMHC/LPC

Carrie Woolman, Mother of a child with autism

Contributions by Jacob Woolman, Father of a child with autism

Foreword by Traci Schneider

The information in this book is designed to provide helpful information for parents and professionals working with children and families with special needs. The content of this book is not meant to be used to diagnose or treat any medical or mental health condition. For diagnosis or treatment of any medical or mental health condition, consult your medical and mental health professional. The publisher and authors are not responsible for any specific medical or mental health needs that may require medical supervision and are not liable for any damages or negative consequences from any treatment, recommendation, tip, point of view, action or application, to any person reading or following the information in this book. References are provided for informational and evidentiary purposes only and do not constitute endorsement of any or by any websites, books, web based articles, scholarly journals or authors.

Published by Compassion Connections, LLC

ISBN: 978-0-9993504-0-9

Dedication

...for the children,
and their parents who love them....

Contents

Foreword

We worried about our child for over 18 long months. Something had to be going on with our son. He wasn't doing what his peers were doing, wasn't communicating, wasn't interacting - and the meltdowns were huge and very long. They lasted for hours! Our pediatrician was constantly telling us that our son was normal, even after many visits and phone calls to their office. What was I supposed to do when Ben melted down for hours at a time? I had another child; an infant; and I was struggling just to make it through the grocery store. After many phone calls, the pediatrician's office suggested I take parenting classes. Needless to say, I stopped calling. I was already feeling like a failure as a mother.

After a long and arduous process, we finally received a referral to have Ben evaluated; however, we had to wait four more months, because the doctor wouldn't test or see him until he was three years old. So, we waited some more. Finally, our son Ben was diagnosed with autism only days after his third birthday.

As parents, this was an extremely difficult day; but it also brought relief. We had already gone through a long and hard-fought journey getting to this point, but now we finally had an answer. The diagnosis allowed us to jump into action to help our son any way that we could. And we did, embarking on hours and hours of intensive ABA therapy, speech, OT, social groups, biomedical approaches, and on and on.

Autism doesn't just affect the child who has been diagnosed. It affects the entire family. Our world was rocked. Our marriage was tested. Our friendships were affected. It changed the life of our younger child. But, no matter how hard it was, it got us to where we are today. We have helped Ben be all that he can be. Autism made our marriage stronger than ever. It made us individually stronger. It made me become a strong advocate. It opened our eyes, and it's taught us so much.

Our son is now 15 years old. He is a sophomore in high school. Ben is our gift. My husband and I always say that he has taught us more than we have taught him; patience being at the top of that list. Ben is a fun young adult. He loves to laugh and be funny. He is really good at building kits, beating people at chess, and rock climbing. He loves to swim, and tolerates taking our dog for a walk every day. He is amazing. He has worked harder in his life to get where he is than anyone I know. He's got a long road ahead of him, but I know he will continue to work hard. That is a gift, and we have to celebrate all of those gifts, big and small.

We have a message for parents of a child with autism: this journey is hard. This journey is long. This journey is one of, if not the most, important things you will do in your life. You can do this. Stay strong, and know the rewards are coming. You are not alone. Find others who understand, and take help when and if it's offered.

Over 12 years ago, after we received Ben's diagnosis, our greatest resource was other parents who had a child with autism. Even though it was sometimes overwhelming to hear their stories, this was so helpful. As we moved forward with all of the various therapies, our ABA therapists became a huge and important part of our lives. Yes, our lives. They were not only there to help our son; they were my lifeline on how to parent a child with autism. I felt empowered. I felt supported. Finally.

I think the collaboration of parent and therapist in this book is a much-needed tool for families not only starting out, but throughout their autism journey. To have both perspectives on the same subjects is brilliant. Our biggest sources of support over the years have come from autism professionals, doctors, and other parents of children with autism.

Autism has touched our entire family. It has become our life and our passion. About six years ago, we were finally at a point in our lives (and in a position) to give back to the autism community. As parents, our hearts were with the other families who were also on the same journey. I met many families over the years; and some of them could not afford all the expensive treatments and therapies to help their child. Is there anything worse than knowing that your child needs help, medical attention, and support; and you can't get it? To know that the state doesn't provide any support or assistance for your child with special needs? To be told that your insurance company does not cover any autism services to help your child get better? This is wrong.

Our hearts are with these families, and that is why my husband and I founded Ben's Fund (www.seahawks.com/bensfund). Ben's Fund is a grant that is available to families in the state of Washington, who have a child with autism. They can apply for financial support for what their autistic child needs the most. We wanted to help these kids and their families directly and immediately. Time is of the essence. Being able to provide this support is such an honor. Being able to do this in Ben's name is incredible. Thank you to Casi and Carrie for donating a portion of the proceeds of this book to Ben's Fund. Thank you to the Seahawks Women's Association, the Seattle Seahawks players and coaches, Families for Effective Autism Treatment of WA (FEAT), and the very generous Seattle community. Without all of you and your support, Ben's Fund would not be possible. Ben's Fund has given over 1,200 grants and counting.

A few closing thoughts...Know you are not alone, even if you feel like it. Stay strong, even when this is so hard to do. Try to take care of yourself, when you can. Ask for help, even if it is difficult. Find the best care and support for your child, especially when these seem like huge mountains to climb. If the door closes or it's not the right one for you, find another door to try. Not everything will work for every child. All of our kiddos are different. If you are in a marriage, try to take care of it. Talk to each other. Communication and respect is what saved our marriage. We lost that, for a little while. When we found it again, we felt like we could conquer anything together. Be there for, listen to, and support your children. Make time for them even when you don't have it. Advocate, advocate, advocate. You know your child better than anyone. It's our job to do anything we can to help them be all they can be. And, no matter what, they will be amazing. Keep up the good work!

I wish you well on your journey. Stay strong!

Traci Schneider

Mom to Ben & Jack
Wife to John Schneider
Co-founder of Ben's Fund
President – Seahawks Women's Association
Board of Directors – FEAT of WA

Introduction

- **An Early Memory**

Carrie (Mother): It was Super Bowl Sunday. My husband Jake and I were having a Super Bowl party at our home. We had several other couples and their kids over to our house for the game. This could have been a very relaxing day for us and a fun day to spend with friends. But it was the day after we received Daniel's autism diagnosis. No one at the party knew our situation. It was a day of confusion and stress and adjustment.

There were several other children at this party, including one boy who was 3 ½ years old, about 1 year older than Daniel. At one point during the party, he came running down the hall from Daniel's room to show his mother an airplane toy we had. He yelled, "Mom, look at this plane!" He got it right in front of her and told her about it. I noticed this interaction and thought, "Daniel doesn't do that. Daniel has never done that."

The comparison phase began for me. A day earlier, we learned the reasons that a diagnosis of autism "fit" for Daniel: lack of eye contact, lack of imitation, lack of pretend play, lack of speech, and aggression. So, I had these reasons on my mind and was now starting to observe children and Daniel differently. The day before, we had also heard some terms for the first time: social smile, cooperative play, joint attention...Daniel didn't do these things. Was it really true? Was Daniel really different? Different enough to receive a diagnosis? This party was the beginning of a new reality for me.

Another moment of pain for me during this Super Bowl party was related to Daniel and biting. Because Daniel had become a biter at about 16 months of age, I knew that he might attempt to bite during this Super Bowl party when we had our friends over. I was stressed out leaving him with other children. I didn't want him to hurt another child, and I didn't want judgment from the other parents if he did bite a child. It caused me a lot of anxiety. All of the other parents just let their children run around the house and play. I should be able to do the same, right? I shouldn't have to follow Daniel around, right?

I tried to act normal. I let Daniel play with the other kids in the bedrooms where all the toys were. However, as I walked from the living room to the kitchen, I could see down the hallway to our bedrooms. Daniel was near this same boy in the hall, and Daniel was clearly getting upset. He wanted a toy that the boy had. They were both in the hall, sitting on the floor. And I thought: "Oh, no! Don't! Please don't bite!" I started running down the hall. Daniel was already lunging for the boy and trying to bite the back of his head! The boy looked at me and yelled out in fear, "He's trying to eat me!" I got to Daniel and picked him up, and I apologized to the boy. There was no serious injury to the other child (and the other parents didn't see...phew!), but it was yet another moment that day where I thought, "Why is this happening? How do we handle this?"

- **Carrie's Goals for This Book**

Carrie (Mother): I remember how surreal it was to receive Daniel's diagnosis. Jake and I decided to tell only close family members and a very small number of friends for the first few months after the diagnosis because we did not feel prepared to answer questions. We didn't understand or know what we were dealing with. In this private time, I grieved and began researching autism. It was a period of isolation. If you are in that same state of mind, of trying to figure out this new world of autism, I hope this book can bring you some comfort and point you in some helpful directions.

I'd like to help shorten the parental learning curve about autism. As Jake and I moved through the months (and years) after Daniel's diagnosis, we gained bits and pieces of information from a lot of different people and sources. I've learned so much, and I'd like to share it with you. So, I'm trying to package up good information, and share it with every newly-diagnosed family.

When Daniel was diagnosed, I ordered lots of books about autism. Some of these books were written by mothers, and some written by clinicians. I read and read and read. Because this book holds the perspectives of both a parent and a clinician, I am hoping it will give a newly diagnosed family more insight into how treatment of their child might progress. Maybe you can read one book (this one) and learn more than you could have gained from reading a handful. I hope to save families some time and money. I hope to help you find a positive "groove" of the services that will work best for you and your child.

I am a better mother because of my experience with autism. I did not want it or ask for it or expect it. But I now cherish it. I have compassion for other families who have children with special needs. I now have a higher level of awareness of the struggles and accomplishments families experience when caring for a special needs child. I want to connect with these families and children. I care about you so much.

My hope is that this book will empower you to keep moving forward in your efforts to support and enrich your child's life. I hope that after you read it, you will feel prepared to speak up and advocate for your child. Each child with autism is so different, and each one deserves many chances to be known and understood. I have learned so much from Casi and others about how to better understand my son, Daniel. I wish that same experience for you: one that is beneficial to your child and your entire family.

- **Casi's Introduction to Autism**

Casi (Clinician): My first encounter with autism began when I was in my undergraduate psychology program. This set the tone for my professional career and my passion for individuals with autism. I distinctly remember that day. I was sitting in my behavioral genetics class in my undergraduate psychology program, when a fellow classmate asked if she could make an announcement. She began with "I work with a family who has a child with autism, and they are looking for another home therapist to work with their son. Is anyone interested?" Hmm, I thought. "Sure, why not?" I said, not knowing that this spur of the moment decision would send me on a professional track that would change my life forever.

At the initial meeting, I met the mom, dad, grandparents, two home therapists who currently worked with the family, and the adorable 4-year-old boy. As introductions ensued, I thought, "These people seem nice. I could do this." They explained how their son's ABA home program worked, who would train me, and the roles of the other therapists. My thought was, "Wow, they have it all together."

Then, there was the little boy, who was running around not making eye contact with anyone, but making lots of noises. As this was my first encounter with autism, I was very intrigued with him, wanting to interact with him, but scared I would do something wrong or make a bad choice and then turn the family off from hiring me...so I just watched him, sat at the kitchen table, and took everything in.

I noticed that this boy did not talk and he did not play with the toys left out for him. How was I going to interact with him? How was I going to teach him things? Am I really capable of learning all this? These were the questions I asked myself; however, there was also an overwhelming feeling of calmness and comfort as I watch the little boy pace from one side of the house to the other, making clicking noises with his tongue.

The one impression that will never leave my mind was that of his parents. The dad was very business-like, direct, to the point, and, honestly, a little intimidating. The mom was softer and very concerned about her boy and wanting him to get the services he needed, but I also sensed a little more of an emotional pull from her...the "mommy gut feeling" was being used when she spoke to me. I could tell she was trying to see if I could have as much compassion for her son as she did; trying to see if I could help him the same way the other therapists could; trying to see if I would be "a good fit" for her son. That day at the kitchen table, in the house by the Puget Sound, meeting with the parents, was when my passion began.

Through the many years I worked with this family, I was privileged to see the ins and outs of how a family operates when they have a child with autism. It may look like they "have it all together" on the outside, like I said before, but inside, they are struggling for themselves and their child. They face many challenges, from medical appointments for sickness and seizures to occupational and speech therapy, behavior therapy team and school meetings to dealing with insurance coverage and out-of-pocket expenses, and battling for a semi–normal childhood for a younger sibling who inadvertently is becoming a caretaker and advocate for her brother.

It astounded me to be there, watching them juggle their schedules and attempt to plan vacations, and to see all the sleepless nights these two people endured. I was even lucky enough to go on a vacation with them, as the therapist helping them keep their son on track with his therapy goals. It amazes me to this day how much this set of parents has gone through to help their child in every way they can. This family also taught me that the only way to help the child is to be on a team with the parents. It is not just about individual therapy; it is about working with the entire family so everyone knows what to do to help the child with autism.

As a result of my work with this family, I can truly value and understand parents when they share their stories. Although each story is different, they all have one common denominator: their love for their child(ren). It has been over a decade since I began on this path, and every day I learn something new about ways to help these children come out of their shells and experience the world.

It is my hope that families and professionals can find a happy middle ground when working together.

For professionals, establishing a middle ground would mean supporting families in a way that takes them outside the box sometimes, listening to their stories and being flexible in the way they provide treatment so that the family system is always taken into account. It would also involve emphasizing in their practice that a large impact can be made by changing just a few small things, keeping the "big picture" in mind but understanding that small baby steps achieve that larger goal.

For families, establishing a middle ground would involve opening up and sharing what your main fears and struggles are so your team of professionals can help you in every way they can. This is so the goals you have for your family as a whole and the goals for your child individually can be met.

I want parents to know that they are not alone; that with help, they really can come through the clouds and feel empowered by the progress and hard work they and their entire team are engaged in. One way this "ideal" relationship is harmed is when professionals say or do things that make families feel like they are not doing anything right, which in turn keeps the family in an eternal state of grieving. The way to avoid this negative outcome is to build communication and trust from the beginning.

- **Casi's Mission with Carrie**

Casi (Clinician): Carrie and I recognized we both want to help families work through the process of figuring out what to do after a diagnosis of ASD (Autism Spectrum Disorder). As a professional, I have a passion for sharing knowledge about children and autism with families, so they are able to learn more about their child and how to establish a successful and nurturing environment. I want to empower them, teach them, and support them in being advocates for their children. These components are directly in my practice name, ETS Therapy Services (Empower, Teach, Support), because my mission is for parents to be able to go from thinking "I don't know how to handle this" to "I CAN handle this. I've got this." Most recently, I have been able to see this mission come to life.

I met with a mother of a child I used to work with when I lived in Seattle. During our conversation, she told me that when I moved away, she was scared. She said I was her crutch and her "go to" person; the one person she knew could help her be sure she was doing the "right" thing for her son. Before I could respond, she continued with how she doesn't feel like that anymore; that I had "taught her well" and given her the tools she needs to feel confident about being a wonderful mom to her adorable and amazing son. This is my mission: for all parents to get to this point in their journey, however long it takes, and to feel like they have control back, instead of feeling that they have no say in how their life with their child will unfold.

I have had many mothers and fathers adopt the methods we spoke about, be an active part of the team, and participate in therapy. This is key. The question still arises, "Why THIS mom - why Carrie and not someone else?" I would say that there is no definitive reason. Carrie and Jake were wonderful to work with, much like many other parents in my case work. But for some reason, Carrie and I shared the same idea, passion, and goal of helping other families by sharing what we have done separately and together. It takes a lot for a parent to share their journey in a public manner; to be absolutely vulnerable. Not just anyone can be a "book writing partner."

So, it was just meant to be; that we came together for Daniel and now we can come together to help other families as well. Unlike other books containing strategies and knowledge about autism and its treatment, this book gives a raw view of both a parent's perspective and a clinician's perspective, under one cover. It provides the newly diagnosed parent with little tidbits of information that can give direction about where to go next - not what should be done. As the parent, it is your choice about what to do to help your child, not ours. We can merely provide you with some choices that have worked for some, but maybe not worked for others. Bottom line: it is your choice.

Chapter 1:
The Evaluations Begin. Could My Child Really Have Autism?

Carrie (Mother): When my son, Daniel, began receiving evaluations for autism, all I knew was that autism was more common in boys than in girls. Other than that, I really did not have much information about autism. As a mother, I wanted to stay away from autism and ignore it. I wanted to squeak through the danger zone and have it be something I would not need to worry about as a parent.

Then, when Daniel was about 17 months old, he started displaying some behavioral characteristics associated with autism. My attitude and ignorance were given an unwelcome overhaul. Maybe you are also facing an upcoming evaluation, or have received an autism diagnosis. This chapter covers some of the attitudes and questions I had about pursuing and receiving a diagnostic evaluation of my son. This chapter also reviews some details from Daniel's actual diagnosis summary.

Casi (Clinician): When most people think about autism, odd repetitive behaviors and social awkwardness come to mind. These characteristics, however, are only a few of the necessary criteria involved in receiving an autism diagnosis. A child diagnosed with autism may be able to talk, make a little bit of eye contact, and have very good attention during the activities in which he/she is interested. Another child diagnosed with autism may have no words, have no eye contact and have significant repetitive behaviors. So, having a diagnosis doesn't mean that your child is going to act just like another child with autism. This is one reason it is difficult, sometimes, to see the areas where a child is struggling. There is not an 'exact comparison' a parent can make to determine if an evaluation is warranted.

- **How to Know Whom to Trust?**

Carrie (Mother): Once your child starts getting into the rounds of developmental and diagnostic evaluations, you may experience that people in your life will want to give you their opinion of the situation. When Jake and I started sharing with family that Daniel was being evaluated for developmental delays, I remember some family members responding with surprise and reassuring me that nothing was wrong with Daniel. I welcomed this feedback. Yet, I continued to take the referrals for further evaluations, hoping that the professionals would also agree that there was nothing wrong. I was kind of just playing along, in my mind.

However, I could have latched onto these opinions of nothing being wrong with Daniel. I could have dismissed the referrals for professional evaluations. I could have disputed external observations and just let Daniel figure things out on his own.

So, who should you trust? What action will you take or not take to learn the truth about your child? I decided that it was strange to have disagreeing parties within my family members, friends, and Daniel's professional care providers. My husband Jake and I continued to seek resolution. My view was that we needed to let Daniel demonstrate to others that he was fine, or not fine, when it came to developmental delays.

Casi (Clinician): The moment you begin meeting professionals and telling friends and family what is going on, you will likely begin to have all sorts of emotions. I always tell any parent I work with that they need to trust their gut instinct and reaction when making decisions about whether to believe, or not believe, someone else's opinion. You know your child the best. It is important to surround yourself with people and professionals that you trust will get to know your child.

Your "team members" are people who will help you make sound decisions that are in your child's best interest. If you don't feel connected or comfortable with a person who is working with your child, your child will not either. This is especially true with a therapist or a clinician. You need to make sure he or she is a good match.

- **Is Your Child Misunderstood?**

Carrie (Mother): Based on your day-to-day interaction with your child, do you find that you are generally the only person who can keep him at peace? That you, essentially, have a special touch. Jake and I felt this way about Daniel. We knew how to read him. We knew how to calm him down. Other people just weren't as good at it as we were. We would have to explain, "No, he likes it like this," or "If you give it to him this way, he likes it better" or "Oh, he's asking for the train." We were his interpreters, and helped him "be" in the world.

Early on, I did feel Daniel was misunderstood by the rest of the world. I felt I was one of a small few who understood him. I knew he was smart. I knew he was sweet and silly. I knew he could be very gentle. However, other people couldn't talk with him. Other people felt ignored by him. Other people saw his tantrums. Other people got bitten by him.

When we began to realize Daniel might have some developmental delays, I decided that I didn't want him to be misunderstood forever. If these services could help him become his own person, able to relate and function properly in the world, I wanted that for him. He was a child who was misunderstood. I didn't want him to grow up to be an adult who was misunderstood.

Do you feel your child is well understood? Can you leave your child with another family member or babysitter with basic guidance, or does it require lots of setup? Can your child adjust to new situations, new foods, new clothes, and new schedules without major meltdowns? Is your child able to express what he or she wants in an effective way (using words and/or gestures) to a variety of people where his requests are understood? I would encourage you to consider how you might answer these questions about your child.

Casi (Clinician): Having a child who is misunderstood is one of many parents' biggest fears for their child. Children with autism are misunderstood on a daily basis, whether it is because of an inability to communicate, a frustration that is illogical and sometimes unknown to others, or an interest in an object or topic that is not shared with other members of their same age peer group. I have heard the phrases Carrie mentions from every parent I have ever worked with. My consistent response is: "How can we help other people understand and communicate with your child, too?" How can we help them feel understood? How can we help them learn ways to feel like they are being heard? Step number one is to give them the opportunity.

- **Do You Fear the Label of "Autism"?**

Carrie (Mother): As a parent, you may be afraid of the label of a disorder. I had this fear. I still have it to a large degree. People may even ask or tell you something like, "Well, you don't want him to get a label, do you?" This can sound so scary and definitive; like your child's life will be over if he gets a label. Is that true? What will happen if he gets a label?

I don't know how the autism diagnosis will ultimately impact Daniel. I have worked to limit any digital footprint that would associate him with autism, but he has the Individualized Education Plan (IEP) with the school district. There is a clear paper trail. And now I'm writing this book. How will this book impact his future? In light of this diagnosis (even if I didn't write this book), could he become a police officer? Could he join the military if he wanted to? Could he be an Olympic athlete (and not in the Special Olympics)? Will kids make fun of him when he is a teenager? I don't know the answers to these questions. If you choose not to seek a diagnostic evaluation, then your child can never get labeled, right? Maybe. Maybe not.

This decision to pursue a diagnosis and subsequent treatment is something you will have to reconcile within yourself. Will you push your child into a zone where they cannot get officially labeled, but also cannot get help? Will you allow your child to get help, if the help may bring along a label of a diagnosis or disorder? Then, you as a parent will be pushed into a new zone of learning, and explaining, and associating with other kids and parents you never thought you would be like.

Maybe, you are like them. Maybe, they are like you, too. On this new road you did not seek, maybe you can make a difference for the better. That is what I'm trying to do with this book. I've learned so much, and Daniel has received wonderful services. These services have undeniably helped Daniel reach a higher potential. I cannot just put those experiences in a time capsule and bury all of that learning and progress. The label may remain for him. What label do you fear?

Casi (Clinician): Throughout my experiences with parents, I have encountered those who were both anxious and excited about the potential of getting a diagnosis for their child. They saw it as a way to fully understand their child and as a potential way to gain more knowledge about what to do next. On the other side of the coin are parents who are terrified of getting a diagnosis of any sort. For them, it is easier to simply "survive" on their own, even in the midst of many challenges. For these parents, seeking out a diagnosis is taking the first step toward a downward spiral of "Now they will never..." comments and a valley of unknowns beyond what was "expected" as a parent. On which side of the coin do you fall?

- **"Meets Criteria" for Autism**

Carrie (Mother): When we were learning more about autism, it was interesting to me to learn the term "meets criteria". Daniel "met criteria" for the autism diagnosis, and so he was diagnosed. Daniel was diagnosed by a clinical psychologist. The diagnostic test used to evaluate Daniel was the ADOS, which stands for Autism Diagnostic Observation Schedule. You can learn more about the ADOS exam on the Autism Speaks website (www.autismspeaks.org). The ADOS primarily evaluates skills in the areas of Social, Communication, and Play.

Excerpts from Daniel's diagnosis report about these three areas of criteria: Some of the observations state he was age-appropriate and behaving typically. I wanted to hang onto these observations more strongly than the ones where he is not displaying typical behavior. However, I had to accept the observations where he was displaying behaviors inconsistent with typical development.

  - Daniel's Social Evaluation

  "Social. In general, Daniel was not interested in engaging in social interaction with the examiner. His eye contact was limited and not typically coordinated with vocalizations. He responded to smiles by his parents by smiling at them a few times over the course of the evaluation. He did not respond to initial attempts by his parents to smile socially or by any attempts by this examiner. Although he directed some of his facial expressions to his parents when upset or happy, Daniel displayed a limited range of facial expressions. During the interaction, Daniel did not demonstrate clear pleasure in interacting with the examiner with the materials but did enjoy interactions with his parents during some activities. Daniel responded to his name being called on the first attempt by the examiner. It was somewhat difficult to gain Daniel's attention, but he did shift his gaze to follow the examiner's gaze toward an object. A nice example of Daniel's social skills was running to his mother for a hug (and smiling) when she returned to the clinic room. During the ADOS, he did not initiate joint attention around an object of interest. He also did not show objects in the evaluation, but did give a pretend phone to his parents to put to their ear. He also brought toys near to his parents but did not turn towards them or make eye contact with them. Daniel enjoyed playing a social game with his parents. Overall, Daniel's social overtures and responses to the overtures made by the examiner were less in quality and quantity than would be expected of his age."

- Daniel's Play Evaluation

"Communication. Daniel used some words during the ADOS, such as "mine", "tuck" for stuck, "help", and "whoa". In general, he vocalized and reached for objects of interest. However, he was observed to combine eye contact with a verbal request for a toy truck. At times, Daniel's vocalizations did not appear directed to others. The intonation, volume, rhythm, and rate of his speech were considered typical. Immediate and delayed echolalia also could not be assessed given Daniel's language abilities. Daniel was observed to use his mother's had as a tool to engage in play with toys. He did not use pointing or other communicative gestures in the session."

- Daniel's Play Evaluation

"Toy play and use of environment. Daniel explored a variety of toys around the room, including the pop-up toy, trains, cars, and a pretend phone. He did not engage in make-believe play with figures but was able to feed a doll some pretend birthday cake. Daniel flicked the eyes of a doll, watch[ed] the wheels of the train roll on the tracks, and felt the texture of the carpet. He did not demonstrate any compulsions or rituals. Daniel demonstrated very brief hand twisting in the session. Daniel exhibited difficulty transitioning between activities and rooms.

He also developed a strong preference for holding cars, a truck and an airplane and became upset when we transitioned to a different activity. Overactivity and anxiety were not observed during the session."

Carrie (Mother): It was in a Saturday morning appointment that we received the diagnosis of Autism Spectrum Disorder for Daniel. We were in the office of the clinical psychologist. She had met with us and observed Daniel the prior Saturday for 2 hours. She met with us again on this Saturday and observed Daniel a bit more before we sat down at an area with couches facing each other. She started walking through her findings. As I often do, I pulled out a piece of paper and took some notes. After she went through some examples of things she had seen or not seen in Daniel's behavior, she told us that she felt "autism was a fit for Daniel". She didn't say "Daniel has autism" or "Daniel is autistic". I think the way she said it was actually very kind and gentle. Her statement conveyed the diagnosis without roughly catapulting him into a new atmosphere of special needs...even though that's where we all arrived.

Jake and I remained calm throughout the conversation. We asked several questions. I remember asking if she thought he was mildly impacted or where she felt he was on the spectrum. And she said "moderate". This was eye-opening to me. Prior to her saying the word "moderate", I thought it must be that he was qualifying with just the slightest enough of criteria that the autism diagnosis could make sense. But when she said "moderate", it made me realize that there are children less impacted by autism than Daniel. With this "moderate" judgement, I realized this was something to take very seriously...even though I just could not yet see all that the clinical psychologist saw in Daniel. In that conversation, I started to become more aware of my own blindspots. I also started to become more curious about why it was so hard for me to see. There seemed to be a lot that I was missing.

Then, the psychologist guided the conversation toward next steps. She gave us referrals to some local providers of ABA Therapy. ABA stands for Applied Behavior Analysis. I had no idea what type of therapy this was, but just that we were being encouraged to get it started. I asked how much therapy we needed. And, I clearly remember her saying that we should be engaging Daniel "every waking hour". That statement was also daunting, just like her word "moderate". She then quantified the therapy part by stating that 25 hours per week should be the goal, but she emphasized that Jake and I could play a role in the therapy and put efforts in place at home to ensure he was "engaged".

One example of engagement that I remember her giving is doing dishes in the kitchen, where Daniel may be on the floor near me. She gave the suggestion of engaging Daniel by putting a soap bubble on his nose, even while just trying to do the dishes. She guided us to find opportunities to engage with Daniel, and request an interaction on a very frequent basis. Keep the interactions going.

After our conversation, we walked out of the office and toward the elevator. I remember Daniel walking and running along beside us. We were both watching Daniel. I looked at Jake. And, I remember Jake saying: "He's going to be fine." I knew that Jake didn't know what he was talking about, but it still made me feel better. Neither of us knew anything substantial about autism. We were going to figure this out together. But we were now at a point where we had to figure out which steps to take next to get Daniel into services.

- **What If You Want a Diagnostic Evaluation and Cannot Seem to Get One?**

Carrie (Mother): Why is it that some health providers are not aggressive about recommending developmental evaluations? I know of families where the developmental evaluation was postponed or families are told to wait and see what happens. If your medical providers are telling you to wait a little longer, you may want to pursue another opinion. It is better not to postpone pursuing evaluations, if not for any reason other than there might be long waiting lists. When you are ready, you may not be able to get an appointment right away.

You can work with your pediatrician to help you assess your child's development. For example, at or near the 18 month well-child visit, you can request the ASD (Autism Spectrum Disorder) screening form. There is a checklist form that they will provide for you to fill out while at the appointment (Screening and Diagnosis for Healthcare Providers, 2017).

If your pediatrician tells you to “wait it out”, and your concerns are not validated, then there are still other options for pursuing assistance.

If you have concerns about your child’s development, it is important to know that any person or parent can refer a child to the local early intervention program. I find this to be commonly unknown. I did not know it when we were starting our evaluations. You don’t need special permission to get an evaluation, but the world of special needs is an unknown world to a new parent.

You or someone else can recommend (or refer) your child for a developmental evaluation. Literally, anyone can make this recommendation such as a childcare center, a grandparent, or a neighbor. The recommendation taps into the “child find” component of the Individuals with Disabilities Education Act (IDEA) (10 Basic Steps of Special Education, 2017). This “referral” can then set into motion a process of more formal developmental evaluations, given parental consent is obtained. To locate your local early intervention agency, try searching online for “early intervention agency”, “child find”, or along with the city name where you live.

Casi (Clinician): Much like Carrie mentioned, it is a common occurrence to have a doctor suggest waiting to see if things continue along an atypical developmental path. If you have a developmental concern, you don’t have to wait. Your child will be better positioned for making progress the sooner you see a practitioner, further evaluate developmental progress, and begin services, if needed.

- **You Will Face Waiting Lists for Services**

Carrie (Mother): It is important for you to learn there are often waiting lists for autism services. You will likely face a waiting list for a formal autism diagnostic evaluation. You may also face waiting lists or very limited availability for specialized therapies or treatments.

Casi (Clinician): One might think that it would not be difficult to get a diagnostic evaluation. On the contrary, as Carrie and Jake experienced, many parents will begin a waiting game once they start seeking the formal evaluation. They may encounter long waiting lists, insurance barriers, or professionals who are not taking new clients. How frustrating and discouraging! These parents are at the point where they reach out to get help and find nothing but barriers. I wish I had the perfect recommendation to parents that would help them avoid this heartache and exhaustive process, but I do not. It is a big issue regardless of where you are located. If you are in a similar situation, I encourage you not to give up, but continue looking for other professional allies to help you work through the process.

- **Choosing the Right Mix of Services**

Carrie (Mother): Also, as Daniel has grown older and gone through new developmental phases, his behavioral needs have also changed. While he may have "graduated" or passed the need for certain services, Jake and I have learned that we will not be "done" with autism for a long time. Maybe never. Absolutely, the mix of services we provide to Daniel has evolved since these early years. I have found it important to periodically evaluate which services make the most sense to guide Daniel's skill development. There are phases where we focus more on academic skills. In other phases we need to emphasize more heavily the social and communication skills.

In Chapter 12, Navigating the Health Care System, I talk more about forming a point of view for services you provide to your child. No one will tell you exactly what you should do, so if your child receives an autism diagnosis, you will have to make some decisions about what services to pursue.

Casi (Clinician): Carrie is 100% correct when she says that they will not be "done with autism." At every developmental stage, there will always be challenges. This is true for all kids; it just looks different for those with an autism diagnosis. At some stages, there will be many areas of challenge, while other stages might have one concern as their primary focus. The bottom line is that a point of view about what is important to your family is key to develop and maintain through all stages of development and life.

- **Can My Child Lose the Autism Diagnosis?**

Carrie (Mother): I find the process of diagnosing autism very interesting because the diagnosis is based on observed behaviors (or lack thereof) in certain areas of life. Autism is not like Downs Syndrome. It is not like Fragile X. The diagnosis of autism is not based on a black and white genetic finding. So, if the autism-specific behaviors decrease, and the age-appropriate behaviors increase, it technically should be possible for a child to stop "meeting criteria" for the autism diagnosis, right? I'm not sure if Daniel will ever stop meeting all ASD (Autism Spectrum Disorder) criteria, but I know that he meets less criteria now than he originally did.

Casi (Clinician): Carrie poses a very important question, "Can my child's diagnosis be reversed?" In order to do that, the child would have to stop meeting criteria for any given mental health condition. Professionally I have known 2 children to do this. This would mean that the child would not demonstrate the necessary behaviors or symptoms that would then qualify them for a diagnosis. All children are different, and their paths of progression are different, so no clinician can answer that question with 100% certainty.

Chapter Summary:

- Is your child able to express what he or she wants in an effective way (using words and/or gestures) to a variety of people, where their requests are understood? If not, keep pursuing evaluations.
- Let your child demonstrate to you (and others) that they are fine or not fine, when it comes to developmental delays.
- This decision to pursue a diagnosis and subsequent treatment is something you may have to reconcile within yourself.
- You will likely face a waiting list for a formal autism diagnostic evaluation and for other services as well.

Chapter 2:
Recognizing a Development Delay

• First Steps Leading to a Developmental Evaluation

Carrie (Mother): When Daniel was 22 months old, Jake and I met with our childcare director and manager upon their request. They told us about a childcare consultation program at a local non-profit organization. They said that they liked to call in representatives from the organization when children exhibited particular behaviors, which the childcare teachers found difficult to handle. It might be helpful to note that this consultation program was delivered through our local "Early Intervention Agency." However, we did not know that term yet. We discuss Early Intervention Agencies (birth to 3 services) in more detail in Chapter 13, Working with Local Services and Schools.

The primary situation with Daniel was that he was biting, and they said he had a "big bubble" regarding personal space. He did not like other kids to enter his bubble. That's when he would bite or hit or get upset. Additionally, they were also concerned that Daniel wasn't very cooperative about sitting in circle time, and he wouldn't line up with the other kids when they were going outside. The childcare director said she wanted to pursue some new tactics in order to help Daniel more effectively. This made sense to us; so we signed the consent form for the childcare consultant to observe Daniel in childcare and provide recommendations.

The first step of the childcare consultation program was an observation, right before Daniel's 2nd birthday. A specialist came onsite to the childcare center and observed Daniel in that setting. We were not present for the evaluation, but we knew it was happening. She conducted her evaluation, gathered her notes, and then we met with her to learn of her findings.

She stated that she had observed Daniel engaging in "visually seeking" activities. This was the first time I ever heard the term "visually seeking". Examples of these types of activities included spinning wheels on a truck rather than rolling the truck through the mud or on a road. She had also observed Daniel put the back of a train to his forehead, and then bend down and roll it on a table, with his forehead still touching the train. It was common behavior for Daniel to lie down to play with his toys even when I knew he wasn't tired. She explained that some of this behavior meant he was watching or feeling how the toys moved rather than actually playing with the toys in pretend scenarios. He focused on specific parts of toys; not the whole toy.

Additionally, in this initial evaluation, the consultant observed that he "mouthed toys" while in the childcare environment. Essentially, he would put toys in his mouth or chew on toys. She explained this response can be caused by high levels of stress. I had never seen this behavior at home, so it was as if they were talking to me about another child, and not Daniel. Was she sure she got it right? Was she sure she was observing the correct child? It was a major disconnect for me. I really thought she must be wrong. However, this was a behavior that was showing up in a different environment for Daniel.

When I started learning that my child was under high stress due to an inability to cope in his childcare environment, it both broke my heart and made me very curious. Why was he under high stress? This was a nice childcare. What was going on? Why was he suffering in a typical environment where many children succeed?

Looking back on this meeting, I am now very thankful to the childcare staff for observing certain behaviors in Daniel that they recognized were not developmentally age-appropriate. As a first-time parent, I did not realize he was slipping behind or dealing with challenges that were out of the ordinary.

Casi (Clinician): The story Carrie tells is one that I hear very often. Parents will report that their childcare center will mention similar concerns: troubling behaviors, lack of social interaction, and behaviors that may indicate a heightened level of stress. Many times, it is hard for parents hear these reports because, like Carrie's experience, they may not see the same behaviors at home. However, it is always good to hear what they have to say. Make your own determinations after hearing all the evidence.

- **Considering a Possible Developmental Delay in My Child**

Carrie (Mother): To me, it seems especially daunting to have your first child face a developmental delay. There are so many emotions

Jake and I went through while learning about Daniel's challenges. We were trying to be good parents, but without the reference point of having had a typical child of our own, we were a bit blinded to some of his delays. I think it is also very easy and tempting to become emotionally defensive of your child and discount third party opinions because you feel you know your child better than anyone. Even though there were several older cousins of Daniel's in the family, whom I had known since their birth, I did not have the knowledge to see the developmental delays in my own son. I am grateful to the childcare providers and the local early intervention program for evaluating my son when they saw reasons for concern. They helped point us in the right direction to find services for Daniel.

Casi (Clinician): I have also heard from many parents that "I didn't know there was something wrong!" Carrie mentioned this same concern. Just as Carrie said, it is so difficult to see your own child's challenges. Along with that, there is grief when the label of "delay" is placed. "I should have known." "I should have brought him/her in earlier." "I should have been able to see how he/she was different than other same age peers." Bottom line: try to take out the "should haves" and focus on your wonderful child and what the next steps are. No parent, first-time or not, is able to be objective with their own child, or to look at them with eyes other than those of a loving parent who wants their child to be perfect. While continuing to grieve for the child you thought you were supposed to have, pair that with some knowledge, forgiveness, and gentle thoughts for yourself.

Most of the time parents are counting on their pediatrician to point out skills their child should have mastered. However, this is not always the case. At times, it is the parent who will bring up concerns over one thing or another, which then lead to deeper developmental questions.

It is helpful for parents to prepare for their 'well child checkups' by looking up the developmental milestones appropriate for the child's current age, so more conversation can be had regarding specific developmental milestones that need to be met. A good resource to determine if a child has met developmental milestones is the Center for Disease Control. Go to their website and click on Autism. A nice chart outlines the specific skills a child needs at certain ages (www.cdc.gov/ncbddd/autism/facts.html).

- **We Were Coping And We Didn't Even Know it**

Carrie (Mother): Before Daniel's additional developmental evaluations and diagnosis, there were several routines that Jake and I developed to help Daniel through his day. Daniel loved apple juice. I didn't leave home without a full sippy cup ready to go, along with a refill. We also knew Daniel loved his trains. We also did not leave home without a metal lunch box full of 8 pieces of wooden track and a few trains. The 8 pieces would form a circle. I would take the trains and set them up for Daniel wherever we went, and he could play and drink his juice. Little did I know that these efforts were parental coping mechanisms, which helped us deal with some of Daniel's behavioral challenges. These weren't things that all parents have to do for their toddlers. These were just things we did that worked for our boy, which kind of "kept the peace".

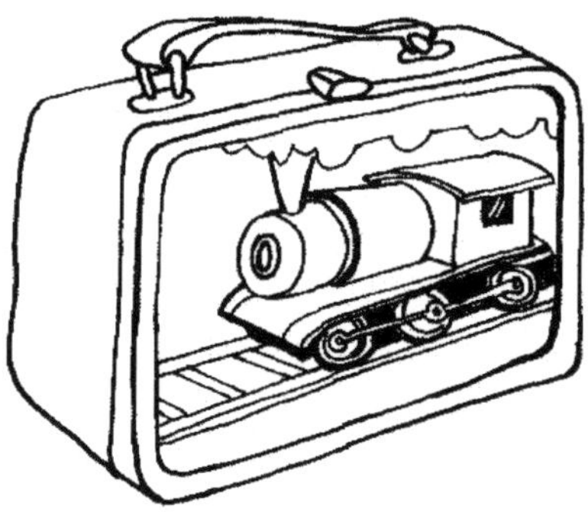

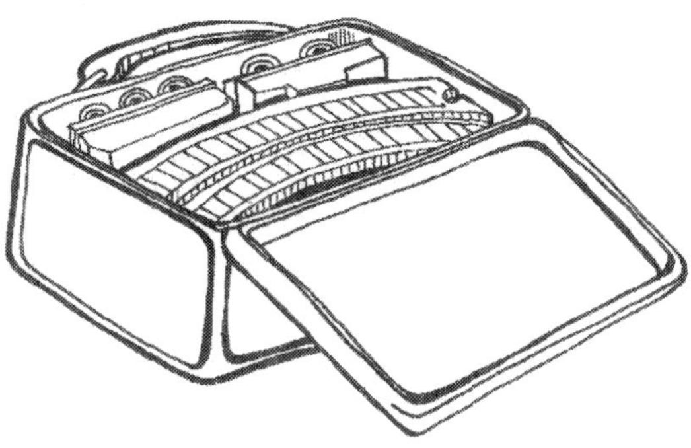

Casi (Clinician): The things Carrie and Jake did to "keep the peace" are not uncommon. In my experience, some parents have used these types of behaviors as coping mechanisms to feel like they are doing what they are supposed to do to make their child happy and feel loved. I have also seen these coping mechanisms used to help calm anxiety when a child's behavior may be challenging and the reasons are unknown. Granted, there are things that all parents do for their children, such as provide a blankie, teddy bear, night light, or a special drink. The main difference between these items and the trains and juice cup Carrie mentions, is that when a reason is given for the absence of the favorite items, neurotypical children can generally calm down. In contrast, children with possible ASD tendencies are unable to do so because they have difficulty with emotion regulation, become easily fixated on favorite items, and may not be able to understand the rationale given.

- **The Concerns From Professionals Continued**

Carrie (Mother): Right after Daniel turned 2, I had Daniel's two-year well baby appointment with his pediatrician. During the typical developmental questions asked in the appointment, our pediatrician asked a few things about what Daniel was doing and not doing. We also shared with him about our current exposure to the local early intervention agency's childcare consultant and that we had a comprehensive developmental evaluation on the horizon. He said he agreed with the direction of getting an evaluation. He also said he was going to give me a referral to a local hospital, and that we could call them to get Daniel more evaluation services. He said that he wanted to caution me because I may start hearing the term "autism," but that nothing was decided yet.

Well, I called the number he gave me, and it went to the Autism Division. Might start using the word "autism"? Yes, I guess so. I was not offended by the suggestion of autism, but realized that what we were dealing with was getting more serious. I was actually fine with going through the motions of an autism evaluation, if that's what the medical community thought was best. However, I tried not to think too much of it. I believed that there was no way Daniel would be diagnosed with something so serious. I was curious to learn more and just get it resolved. I also wanted to do the best for my son, and I wasn't going to deny him the opportunity to be seen by specialists.

Over the course of Daniel's 3rd year (between age 2 and 3), Jake and I had many different evaluations. They came from our pediatrician, two local autism clinics, a clinical psychologist, the local Birth to 3 early intervention program, and the childcare provider. It's hard to argue with several different evaluations when they all tell you similar things.

Casi (Clinician): When professionals express concern is expressed regarding a child, it is so important to have multiple people's input about what the child is doing in each separate environment. Communicating with childcare providers, teachers, afterschool care, grandparents or friends that watch the child can be an important strategy to grasp the "big" picture of where the child is at in comparison to his/her same age peers. The development of an open and honest "check in" routine that cycles through each environment can be a helpful tool. When a difficult behavior or concern is brought up, it can be hard to digest what is said. However, it can be an open door to finding the right services for the child.

- **Daniel's First Comprehensive Developmental Evaluation**

Carrie (Mother): The comprehensive developmental evaluation at the local early intervention agency occurred when Daniel was 26 months old. The evaluation was given by with an early intervention team, evaluating Daniel in the skill areas of Adaptive, Expressive Language, Receptive Language, Cognitive, Social/Emotional, Gross Motor, Fine Motor, Vision, and Hearing.

The session got off to a bit of a rocky start. On the way to the examination play room, we passed another room that had a train table. Bad news. Daniel saw it and wanted to play. The fact that we had to go to a different room was not an acceptable option to him. So, we started off the meeting with a meltdown. I told them I'd brought juice, and would they mind if I gave it to him? I got out my trusty juice cup and set up those 8 wooden track pieces. After several minutes, Daniel calmed down. I remember the evaluation team complimenting me on knowing how to calm Daniel. I thought that was a bit of a strange comment. Was what I was doing unusual? I didn't verbalize these questions and doubts. I just smiled and said, "Oh, thanks".

The evaluation team got started. They worked over the next hour to engage Daniel in a variety of activities, asking him to imitate certain things or engage in certain play activities.

In the summary of the comprehensive evaluation, these are some of their observations:

1. Daniel does exhibit sensory processing challenges which are impacting his overall development
2. Recommendation to follow up with an eye care professional to check Daniel's vision (due to his light sensitivity)
3. Daniel's expressive language skills are below the expected range for his age
4. Daniel's receptive language skills are below the expected range for his age
5. Daniel's cognitive skills are within what is expected for his age
6. During the evaluation, he preferred to follow his own agenda, and it was difficult to redirect or engage him in a therapist's choice of activity
7. Daniel's social skills are below what is expected for his age.
8. He inconsistently responded to his name and sounds in the environment during the evaluation
9. Daniel's gross motor skills are within what is expected for his age
10. Daniel's fine motor skills are slightly below what is expected for his age

With the comprehensive evaluation complete and his results summarized, the early intervention team recommended speech therapy and occupational therapy for Daniel.

- **Daniel Begins Therapy**

Carrie (Mother): One aspect of the local early intervention program is that they were not a diagnostic facility at the time they worked with Daniel. I have learned that they do now provide some diagnostic services for autism, which is a wonderful addition. However, at the time Daniel was being evaluated for developmental delays, the early intervention agency could not diagnose him with a disorder. Instead, they measured developmental progress and treated the developmental delay. We did not have an answer yet about the autism question. The autism diagnostic appointment was still almost two months away.

Nevertheless, we began speech therapy and occupational therapy with the early intervention agency right away, within the same month of his comprehensive evaluation. He was 26 months old, so he was eligible for 10 months of services before he turned three years old. I wanted to pack in as much therapy in that period much as we could.

The therapy sessions were immediately helpful to Daniel, and educational to Jake and me. As these therapists started working with Daniel, we learned they could conduct their sessions in the childcare environment instead of only at the clinic. This was an amazing service for two main reasons.

First, it allowed Daniel's therapy to progress even while Jake and I were at work. This was a benefit to me because I knew that Daniel was getting good therapy even when Jake and I could not be there. Second, it gave another perspective on Daniel's original childcare setting. Because of some of the observations from the onsite therapist, we realized that the current childcare might not be the best place for him, since the agenda was not very structured. Her observations helped us pursue a more suitable childcare environment for Daniel.

We found a new childcare center with a more structured agenda, and we decided to register Daniel. Fearing rejection, I was anxious about sharing the information about Daniel's biting, his developmental delay information, and his upcoming autism diagnostic appointment. To our great relief, the childcare teachers were very compassionate and willing to implement the specific accommodations Daniel now required (like visual cues and modified responses to his biting). Additionally, we arranged for the local Birth to 3 (early intervention) therapists to continue delivering therapy onsite at this new childcare center.

This new childcare arrangement all began just prior to Daniel's diagnosis, but it was one major step towards us finding a "groove" of services and a new environment for Daniel that might bring him some relief in a world that was causing him so much adversity and stress.

Chapter Summary:

- Daniel's childcare provider was the first group to help us understand that Daniel might be experiencing some developmental delays. They connected us to our local Early Intervention Agency (birth to 3 services) for an initial consultation.
- Our pediatrician and the Early Intervention Agency reinforced the childcare team concerns about Daniel's development and behavior.
- Daniel began initial speech therapy and occupational therapy at 26 months of age, and he (and we) began experiencing some improvements from this help.

Chapter 3:
How Will You Respond to the Diagnosis?

- **What Caused the Autism in My Child?**

Carrie (Mother): Good question. I encourage you to look at different causation models that medical professionals propose as the possible cause of autism (McCandless, 2009). Many sources outline possible causation models for autism. You can review the details and determine if any of them seem to ring true based on your child's experience. What they really show me is that there is currently no known true cause.

This lack of a definitive cause of autism is something that gave me a lot of hope that perhaps Daniel's conditions and behaviors might improve over time or with therapy. At first, the diagnosis can feel like a "dead end" message, depending on how that message is delivered. As I learned more about causation theories and other families' successes, this knowledge gave me energy to pursue options that painted a very different picture than that of a "dead end".

- **Stages of Grief**

Casi (Clinician): Once the realization happens that something more serious could be going on rather than a mere toddler/developmental phase that all kids go through, there can be a time of grief. This should not be confused with the grieving process that begins when a diagnosis is given. The grieving process in this initial realization step is more about that unknown component of their child that causes surprise and devastation. During this phase, I have seen parents research other types of disorders or issues their child could be showing symptoms of, deny that anything is wrong, attribute their behavior to a sickness or stage of life, withdraw completely from family, and get angry at anyone who suggests something other than what they want to believe. It is important for each family member to understand that grieving is a natural and important process that everyone must go through. This information is important because I have seen grief paralyze a family to the point that they never get the help they need, both for their child and for themselves.

After the initial shock that something is wrong, the official grieving process starts. Grieving begins when something you had is lost, or something you wanted is no longer obtainable. For parents, this loss is of the child you thought you were going to have. Let's take a look at the stages (Kubler-Ross & Kessler, 2014).

1. Denial and Isolation

In this stage, parents are in denial that anything is wrong. Sometimes this happens before the official diagnosis, and sometimes after. I am sure every parent can remember when this occurred for them: they want to isolate themselves from all the other children and parents and just stay home with their children and immediate family. Reality is not present during this stage; it is just too hard to accept.

2. Anger

Whose fault is it? Who can I blame for this happening to my child? These are questions parents ask when going through the anger stage. They are so mad that this is happening. Someone has to pay, and be blamed for it, because that would mean this unpredictable situation would make more sense.

3. Bargaining

"If only we got to the doctor earlier." "If only we had watched for signs." Maybe if I say we will never take our life for granted again, this will go away." These thoughts are common in this stage of grief as they try to make deals with whomever or whatever they can to make their life different. For some parents, looking back and focusing on the things they didn't do, and giving those as reasons as to why this is happening to their child is a way to make sense of the whole thing.

4. Depression

During the depression stage, there are two types of depressive states parents go through: the sadness and regret stage, and the quiet, private, being alone stage. Both stages have to pass before getting to the final stage of grief. The sadness and regret can look like a parent who is sad for their child and wishes things could be different. The private part is when parents withdraw and become very quiet and keep to themselves, not allowing anyone to really help them when all they need is probably a silent hug.

5. Acceptance

Acceptance is the final stage, where moods and mindsets are changing. When parents hit this stage, it is all about saying "ok, this happened, it is not what I expected, but I can move forward."

The stages do not need to go in order, there is no time limit to each stage and stages can be skipped and repeated as needed as the loss is processed. A person can stay in a stage for a short or long amount of time; all depending on that individual. Sometimes stages can be revisited, at a later point in time long after the initial loss, as the development process progresses and new challenges arise for their children. It is an ever-evolving process that I encourage parents to be open about. It needs to happen.

- **My Response to the Diagnosis**

Carrie (Mother): It's a little awkward to go back and try to put my emotions into the nice little buckets of the five stages of grieving, but I think I can do it to some degree. In this section, I review how I felt, changed, and learned as I adjusted to having a child newly diagnosed with a special needs challenge.

1. My Denial

As a new parent, and one that was now facing caring for a child with developmental delays, I found myself swirling in a fog, trying to put one foot in front of the other and trying to get the best care for my child. There were steps that Jake and I took to keep moving forward, and we found services there for the taking. We just had to reach out to get them. I've heard that a lot of parents do not reach out. They shield themselves with denial or some other blocking force and move forward without help.

I did not believe that Daniel was as "bad off" as the diagnosis made it sound. I decided I was willing to "play the game" of getting services just to prove them wrong. I was trying to grapple with the diagnosis and trying to accept it, but I just could not fully label him. I felt like I was lying when I would say my child has autism. I was caught between believing and not believing. So I went along with the services. I wanted the services because I didn't trust my own judgment. I wasn't going to deny him services that experts said he qualified for.

2. My Anger

My denial turned to anger. I can best explain some of the anger and frustration I felt by re-living our first introductory meeting with Casi. About 1 month after Daniel's diagnosis appointment, we had our first meeting with Casi. It was at a leading autism services provider in the Pacific Northwest. I met up with Jake from work. I was on the verge of tears even walking through the buildings to get to the meeting room. It was a typical March day in the Northwest; mostly overcast. I remember the facility was doing construction and there were all these weird makeshift covered walkways we had to navigate from building to building. We navigated them first to the main office. Casi came and met us and led us back through the covered walkways to another building where the therapy rooms are. The covered walkways zig-zagged and were unstable. They were annoying and frustrating to me: kind of symbolic of this new journey Jake and I were starting with Daniel; a difficult, frustrating, and uncertain path. I just walked behind Jake, thinking put one step in front of the other. We made it to the therapy room. It turned out to be the therapy room we would be in for most of the ABA sessions Daniel would have with Casi.

Since Daniel was not at this introduction appointment, we brought a photo book of Daniel to show Casi pictures of our son, to make him more human to her. He was our little boy, now caught in this storm of a diagnosis of a mental disorder. A mental disorder was not in my plans for my son. I knew my son. He was so sweet and cuddly and precious. No. I reject it. I reject that he has a mental disorder. However, I had a six-page diagnosis to battle. So, why wasn't he counting at 28 months? Why was he biting? Why wasn't he talking as much as other kids his age? Why did he lay down to play even when he wasn't tired? Why did I have to pack juice and trains with every outing just to "keep the peace"?

In our first meeting with Casi, I do not remember all that was said. However, I was raw emotionally and wanted Jake to do the talking. I remember chiming in and starting to talk, and then I broke down. I tried to explain how the diagnosis had gone. I can now rattle off the top five things Daniel struggled with which qualified him to "meet criteria" for the autism diagnosis.

1) Lack of speech
2) Lack of eye contact
3) Lack of pretend play
4) Lack of imitation
5) Aggression

I was not yet at the point, in this Casi meeting, of having this top five list. I didn't understand how our boy had autism. I did not understand. I was angry.

Additionally, I felt anger as a result of some of the fast improvements Daniel made when we changed his diet. I could not help but become angry at the health system and angry at myself. I feel like I let my son get f&*@$d up. It was my fault. How could I have been so blind? If I had only known these things when Daniel was a baby. If I had only known to give probiotics when he was on antibiotics. For reasons most women would know, because he was a boy, I didn't think to do this. If he had been a girl, I would have asked. His one-year well child checkup revealed no developmental delays. So – what went wrong? What happened between 12 months and 28 months?

Casi (Clinician): I was so excited to meet Carrie and Jake that day. From reading Daniel's file, I knew he was young and newly diagnosed. A little one with so much potential, I thought to myself. When I went into the waiting room and called out their names, Carrie's facial expression was that of a stunned and grieving mother. My heart was heavy for her. We sat at the table and I started with my usual "So tell me about Daniel." I remember Carrie trying to start the conversation with Daniel's struggles, but she immediately shut down, red eyes rimmed with tears. Jake stepped in from there and continued to explain what their concerns were and what they cherished about their boy. They described the train box and juice cup, which were items they needed to have with them at all times. I knew this process was going to be difficult for them because of the intense coping skills they had developed. "I need to get these parents out of survival mode and help them realize this is not the way they have to live," is the thought that crossed my mind. But, it needed to start with them.

They took out the picture book they'd brought with them, giving me a face to put with Daniel's name. They showed me a list of words Daniel could say. I asked them if he would use these words to ask for things he liked or disliked. Their response was, "Well, yes, he says them." In my mind I was thinking, "Okay, he is not using these words to functionally communicate his wants and needs." They were not ready for it. I also remember them asking me if I had a child of my own, which I do. I was hesitant to answer; however, I was not going to lie to them. Why was I hesitant? Because then it was about me and my child instead of about them and their child.

Carrie (Mother): At this point, Jake and I were looking for people who might understand the grief we were experiencing. If Casi answered that she didn't have any children, it would not have stopped me from having her work with Daniel. However, when she shared that she had a son who was actually younger than Daniel, it made me feel like she might understand the stress and fear of trying to raise a healthy, happy child. So, I appreciated that she shared that she had a child, and specifically a boy.

3. My Bargaining

I don't remember going through a whole lot of bargaining. But what I do remember is setting goals for myself and Daniel that I would pour into him before he was five. Because of many things I read, I started to feel like I was now on a "ticking clock". That Daniel had until he was five to make as much improvement as possible was a pressure that I was now under, to help him fulfill. I thought, "Okay, we still have some time. I'll make this work and do everything I can to undo the damage already inflicted...to redeem myself."

4. My Depression

As I began realizing that the dietary changes were helping Daniel so much, I started feeling very foolish for not being more aware of these nutritional and physiological realities. I should have paid more attention. I started grieving that Daniel was not my "test-case" for a son. He was not meant for me to "learn" on. My first child was suffering from the lack of knowledge of his first-time parents. I was overwhelmed with a feeling that I had let him down. I apologized to him over and over. I was so sorry. He was not just something for me to learn from, so that I could do things better with our next child. I needed to get into action and do better by him. Trusting the "system" was no longer good enough. Leaning on other people's expertise was failing my son. This realization has caused me to often term him as the collateral damage of western medicine. He was falling through the cracks in the system.

I also remember just crying all the time during this period of time, my depression phase. During the first 3-4 months after the diagnosis, we didn't tell many people beyond close family about the diagnosis. I didn't want to have to try to answer questions. I had no idea what to say. So, it was a time of isolation and visible grief. I kept a box of tissues in my car, and stayed very upset.

During this period of time, we were still utilizing the early intervention agency services; but now post-diagnosis. I attended one of their information sessions about services in local school districts. I distinctly have this memory which was most likely during my depression phase of grief. My mother-in-law attended the session with me. Jake was home with Daniel. It was just a few weeks after Daniel's official diagnosis. I was still a mess, and couldn't help but cry most of the session. I looked around at other parents, and no one else was crying. I wondered how they were so comfortable with their children's situation. I was wondering what everyone else was dealing with. Why was I the only one visibly upset? This bothered me.

After the session, I spoke with the facilitators, one of whom was a senior member of the staff for our school district's pre-school. In a blubbering way, I told her we were recently diagnosed. She was very understanding and kind. No judgement. I greatly appreciate that night. I suppose I was in the darker spot of my depression phase. And I felt very confused and just different from everyone else...even the other parents in the room who were in a similar situation to me. We were all trying to navigate the new world of caring for a special needs child.

5. My Acceptance

The lack of a social smile and using my hand as a tool were the two main items that convinced me that my son was on the spectrum. I could not deny these behaviors. Other behaviors where he fell short included not responding to his name appropriately, and not making eye contact appropriately. Now, understanding how to watch for these behaviors was a new level of enlightenment for me; like when you can sense a new level of understanding that you did not possess before. It's like when you can shed layers of "protection" that were not really protecting you, or like being pulled through a barrier without your consent, not realizing that the barrier had previously boxed you in. This was not a welcome enlightenment for me. It completely changed how I saw Daniel. I know this is a common response from parents whose children are diagnosed. It is the dawning of a new understanding that you might rather give back; but you cannot. There is more to see, more to know, more to respond to, and more to prepare for.

Casi (Clinician): During a diagnostic evaluation, parents are asked many, many questions about their children's skill level and developmental progression. When this occurs, a vast majority of parents are surprised at how many behaviors or lack of demonstrable skills are of concern in the eyes of the examiner. As in Carrie's example, when a child uses another person's hand as an extension of their own (using another's hand as a tool) parents think, at times, that it is their child's way of communicating their wants and needs and showing affection towards that person. While this can be partially true, it also indicates that the child does not have the ability or knowledge to communicate in a more age-appropriate way, such as using words or pointing. Many times, children see another person's hand as an extension of their own and not attached to another person.

Another frustration expressed by parents has been that their child did not show the examiner or clinician the skills they do at home or with familiar people. This then indicates to the parent that the examiner did not get an accurate picture of their child, and therefore the diagnosis is invalid or inaccurate. Although it is common for children to act differently from one environment to the next, it is typically not enough of a behavior change to indicate different levels of skill. When a child shows an examiner many areas of skill deficits in the clinical setting, it signals to the clinician that the child does not have the ability to consistently exhibit the skills needed to function appropriately in their environment. With that said, there should always be parent input involved in any diagnostic assessment because the parent does know more about their child than a professional ever will. -A good diagnostic assessment takes the clinical observations noted in the assessment as well as the parent report of behavior into account when placing a diagnosis on a child.

- **Glasses You Can't Take Off**

Carrie (Mother): I view this new level of enlightenment given by the autism diagnosis as though it's given you glasses you cannot take off. I hated those glasses, at first. I didn't like seeing what I was quickly learning were atypical behaviors in Daniel. Once they were pointed out to me, I couldn't un-see them. I could not help but see my child differently. Potentially quirky things about him were now related to the diagnosis.

There were aspects of Daniel's behavior that I had to accept as atypical. I started learning about the difference between parallel and cooperative play, and that Daniel was not participating in cooperative play. I started learning about self-stimulating behavior (flapping hands, moving toys in unusual ways, spinning in circles), and then began observing those behaviors in Daniel. I started learning about high stress behavior in my child, such as mouthing toys and having a "big bubble" when it came to personal space. I realized that Daniel should be pointing, but he rarely did. I learned that 2-year-olds generally have "messy" bedrooms or toy rooms because of active play, but Daniel's room stayed tidy.

As we moved through the next few weeks and months, trying to wrap our arms around the diagnosis, I went through the process of releasing my expectations about Daniel. I released the things I felt he could or should do in his life, like going to college, driving a car, moving out of our house, playing sports, getting married, or other typical life events. This process of releasing my expectations for him gave me a blank canvas on which to see Daniel. My new hopes for him were to simply help him achieve whatever potential he did have. Our new job, as his parents, was to discover the potential he had; but even then, I didn't feel that we needed to pressure this potential. I wanted to help him achieve his best self and take barriers out of his way that might make him stumble. I began to feel the true sense of wanting the best for my child without my own agenda getting stamped on him. I now really appreciate this process that I went through. Jake would describe it to me as realizing that Daniel would simply be his buddy; perhaps for the rest of our lives. Daniel would be ours, and we would help him. We would help him move through the world.

- **My Original Daniel and My New Daniel**

Carrie (Mother): In adjusting to Daniel's diagnosis, it was as though I had to introduce myself to this new child I had never met before. I had expectations and goals for my original Daniel. This Daniel, under the umbrella of the diagnosis, was someone new to me. I had to re-learn him like I did when he was a newborn. I had to let him be redefined through new lenses and from different points of view. Then, I had to shape my new understanding of him. I could not hold on to my old one. This was not a child who would respond to timeouts. This was not a child who was just stubborn. He was no longer a child whom I could just expect to progress like all my friends' children. I had to engage with him at a new and unfamiliar level. I had a lot to learn.

- **Collapse of My Vision for My Son**

Jacob (Father): I think there is a different excitement for a dad becoming a father to a boy than there is for a girl. It is obviously not good versus bad, it's just different. This is how I would explain it, for me: You take what you know of yourself; the good and the bad. You start to digest it all once you find out that you are going to have a baby boy. Then, you start to sift through all the memories of being a child yourself. You create a perfect scenario for your boy, whether it be the activities you liked, the sports you played, the kind of friends you had, or the experiences you had in elementary, junior high and high school. All of this gets encapsulated in what you start to see for your son. I think it is a very normal way that a father is allowed to "nest" for their new baby boy.

I am talking about my son, in my case, but I also feel that the process would have been similar if I'd had a girl. The dynamics just would have shifted to include a whole different set of hopes and dreams for raising a daughter, all just as important and exciting but different. Nonetheless, when you have created the perfect plan for your son, whether it will ever play out the way you imagined or not, the vision is there for your child as you think about his upcoming life. The collapse of my vision for my son happened so much earlier than I think most fathers have to confront. At the age of 28 months, when my son first was diagnosed with ASD, the train in my life derailed and my vision for him was the casualty, along with countless of other pains and hurts that have been left in the wake of the devastating news. It is very hard to catch your breath after news like that, let alone think about what life would hold for our lives as parents now. More importantly, what would life look like for my son?

However, not to be left without hope, our journey has seen more victories than I could have ever imagined.

- **My Son Might Not Be Like Me**

Jacob (Father): In my adjustment to the diagnosis, I had the feeling of realizing that my son might not be like me. It is like letting go of all you had planned for him to do in his life. I had to put aside expectations and move past the heartache of possibly losing what I wanted him to do or be. I realized that he will shape the path, and I will travel with him not him traveling with me. I began the process of attaching myself to his interests and passions. It was about surrender, for me.

On parenting in general, I do not think this process of surrender is necessarily ASD specific. I think any time your dreams and hopes for your child fade away for a variety of possible reasons, this change to your vision for them can be just as difficult to endure.

- **The Perceived Pressure of a Time Crunch**

Carrie (Mother): I did quickly develop a fear that Daniel was running out of time to achieve his early childhood development milestones. I was afraid that at 28 months of age, we may have caught on to Daniel's challenges too late to address them. Professionals reassured me that he still had time, but I was not sure what to think.

I've since learned that Daniel received a very early diagnosis compared to a lot of children. I've since met parents who did not receive a diagnosis until their child was 4 years old or older. I'm now very thankful for the relatively early diagnostic evaluations we received, but we still had to wait for them once we knew they were warranted. Many other parents are still waiting or are not receiving appropriate referrals for evaluations.

Casi (Clinician): As a clinician, I feel it is very important to receive intervention as soon as possible. However, I also think that, much like Carrie's feelings, parents hear about this "window" of time and therefore feel that they have missed out, or experience a sense of guilt or failure. As a behavioral clinician, I feel that behavior can be changed and skills can be learned at any point in a child's development. Yes, the earlier the better; but that doesn't mean all hope is lost. It is my opinion that as soon as you receive that diagnosis, it is a good idea to start the journey towards finding the right combination of services for your child. It is never too late.

- **Your Identity as a Parent**

Jacob (Father): Your identity can get lost in the dreams you have for your child. When you see those dreams slowly fading because of the circumstances you face, it is very hard to rebuild and move down the new life path which has been put before you. "Digging deep" is a total understatement for me. I experienced a total overhaul of how I saw my life, my child, and my future. I had to rebuild my identity with something that was so hard to accept.

I tried to keep my identity as close to what I had always been while allowing my son to form his own identity without any limitation. I still had to take on this new challenge of what it meant to have a child with autism. This experience would be woven into who I was moving forward.

- **New Terms: Typical and Atypical**

Jacob (Father): The term many people use and accept now is that "diversity" is completely acceptable, which means that we are all "different" in our own unique way. Great, I agree. No two people are alike. I get that; but what is hard to swallow are the terms "typical" and "atypical". "Atypical" is how kids on the spectrum are referred to when compared to kids who are not. So, you can be different, but typical or atypical and different. So take away the word "different", and you are left with typically functioning kids or atypically functioning kids.

The degree to which your child is different when comparing typical and atypical kids is much more stigmatized than just saying we are all different in our own unique way. It makes me feel like there is a failure of mine involved somewhere, and that feeling brings heartache and loss. It brings with it a sense of some form of failure on the parent's part. It is an extremely heavy burden to bear because blame automatically sets in about what I did wrong. I asked myself, "How come I didn't see this happening?" It is a dark conversation I have with myself which eats at my very being because I see a part of myself in my child, who is struggling to be understood, accepted, or even looked at in a respectful, normal way. Every fiber in my body aches for typical, for normal, because of the greatness I see in my young child who is trying desperately to express himself, but who struggles to do so because of the way his body and mind have let him down.

- **Daniel as My Buddy**

Jacob (Father): At some point after receiving the diagnosis, I remember arriving at a new peace and forming a different approach related to Daniel. I remember a conversation Carrie and I had when I said that it was okay if Daniel was just going to be my little buddy for life. If that was how all this was going to play out for us, it would be okay. It seemed as though I had to come up with the worst-case scenario and had to accept this new, alternate reality because of the diagnosis. Once I came to terms with what the diagnosis meant for my family and me, it began to feel like my victory. So, my worst case scenario never truly felt like a "worst case" as we continued to walk through this journey. I had overcome my fears and found strength in knowing that whatever my little boy needed, I could and would provide a great life for him regardless of how much or how little progress he made.

- **Autism as My Adversary**

Carrie (Mother): As we started in with therapies and dietary changes, I would sometimes be caught off guard by autism's grip on Daniel. It was smothering him, I felt, and I had to try to loosen its grip on him. I had to battle this invisible enemy that was hiding my "true" child from me. As Daniel started making progress in his therapies, I grew angry at this enemy. I felt I was fighting for Daniel, and autism would sometimes make a fool of me. I often felt autism (personified) was laughing at me.

For example, when Daniel was about 3 years old, he had learned his animal sounds; meaning, he could answer "What does a dog say?" and "What does a cow say?

I thought he knew all his animal sounds, but one night I asked him the reverse question about a variety of animals, and he could not answer any of them. Is there a difference in the knowledge needed to answer these two questions: "What does a kitty say?" versus "What animal (who) says "meow"?" These questions are not very different, but Daniel would only be able to answer the first question when he was about 3 years old. This really bothered me. Daniel could answer with sounds associated with the animals, but he couldn't answer the question in reverse. This was a sign of memorization, not learning.

Making these types of discoveries really bothered me. This is when autism would reach out of the darkness and slap me on the face, punch me in the gut, push me down to the ground, and remind me "I'm still here. I've still got a hold on your child. What you thought was progress was a trick from me. Your child is good at memorization, not learning. Your child is faking it to please you. No - not even to please you; but just to get his needs met. You're a fool." Autism's mockery is silent, bitter, and very shrewd. Well played, autism, well played. You are a worthy adversary, whom I will not underestimate. Time to get some new weapons against you. You're pissing me off.

- **My Son is Diagnosed with Autism**

Carrie (Mother): It is difficult for me to say, "I have an autistic son". So, I don't say that. I generally say, "my son was diagnosed with autism". I suppose my main reason for this is that I don't want autism to completely define Daniel. Saying he is "autistic" casts a cloak around him that somehow makes it so final, such an open and shut case. And, it is just not that simple. There are some areas of our life or times throughout our day where autism in Daniel is not a major factor. Yet, it is always present. Jake and I have shaped our parenting within and under the cloud of autism. My son is more than "autistic", yet he is diagnosed with autism. This nuance makes a big difference to me in the way I speak about my son, when I choose to speak about the diagnosis. And, I don't always choose to speak about the diagnosis.

- **Becoming an Advocate for Your Child**

Carrie (Mother): As Jake and I continued to take Daniel to his multiple evaluations and therapy sessions, we began receiving guidance about how to be better advocates for Daniel. He was going to need us to be his advocate. I began to adopt this mindset, and I paid attention to the suggestions.

One example of advocacy is to bring a picture of your child when meeting with a potential new provider. I was given the advice of just helping the provider or administrator put a face with a name (if they don't already know your child). This advice is the reason I brought a little picture book of Daniel the first time Jake and I met with Casi.

Casi (Clinician): A large part of my professional mission is to empower parents to advocate for their child. This can look differently from parent to parent, therefore I have no exact recipe for what it entails. The main goal is to help and support your child in whatever way feels most comfortable. We discuss a few ideas in this chapter, however the suggestions are not 'must do's" of being an effective advocate. Find the way that feels right to you.

- **Gathering My Documents and Resources**

Carrie (Mother): With a variety of developmental and health evaluations you might be experiencing, I suggest purposefully keeping track of the information and documents providers will share with you. I found that I often had to reference certain documents or assessments for new providers. Especially if you are still having difficulty accepting the reality of the diagnosis, try to set up a bucket, a shelf, a drawer, a binder, where you can put all the paperwork regarding your child. These include your child's medical exams, assessments, prescriptions, books, community resources, and contact information of professionals. Of course, you can keep a lot electronically on your computer, as well. Just start putting it all in one place, for quick reference.

- **Beginning a Journal**

Carrie (Mother): You may also want to start a journal where you can keep track of symptoms and progress in your child based on whatever interventions or treatments you are trying. For me, in the early months after Daniel's diagnosis, the days went by very slowly, and Daniel's progress seemed sluggish. As I've been able to look back at the notations I've made, especially in those first few months, I realize that the progress Daniel made was actually very fast from everyone else's perspective or from a normal frame of time.

Keeping a journal or a place to log progress (or lack of progress) is something I'm very thankful I did. I wish I had noted more, but I cherish what I do have. The last thing you need is more pressure of another thing to do, but having these journal entries about my emotions and Daniel's progress is one of my most prized possessions. It also helps enable me to share with you the positive outlook I'm now able to have. I'm perhaps just a few years ahead of you, in your journey with autism, but I want to help you walk the path. All that I've been through with Daniel has turned me into a better mother for him (and now, for Caleb, our second child).

Casi (Clinician): Many times parents are either frustrated by the lack of progress, or forget how much progress their child has made! These are two reasons why it is important to write down some of the more significant gains and challenges that your child has demonstrated over the years. I have found that it is easy for parents to forget some of the interventions and strategies they have used with their child to make progress. Journaling about everything is thus important to gain perspective, lift spirits, and for peace of mind.

Chapter Summary:

- What Caused Autism in My Child? There is no definitive answer, but tracing back health and development milestones may help you seek the appropriate services for your child.
- Upon receiving the diagnosis, you may experience grief. Give yourself permission to grieve the loss of your previous understanding of your child as you begin to embrace a new one.
- Try not to get stuck in denial. Your child needs you to act on their behalf.

Chapter 4:
Fundamentals of ABA

- **Applied Behavior Analysis (ABA), or Behavior Therapy**

Casi (Clinician): In a nutshell, Applied Behavior Analysis (ABA) is the systematic way we teach a specific skill to a child. It is broken down into parts so the child can understand the expectations (Cooper, Heron & Heward, 2007).

This chapter is meant to give you an idea of what ABA therapy is, how it works, and how it looks when watching it. This is in no way an all-encompassing account of ABA; just a few bits of information to get you thinking about this way of teaching children with autism.

There are a few variations of ABA; two of which are highly structured Discrete Trial Training (DTT) and Naturalistic forms of ABA. Highly structured methods of ABA utilize a consistent instruction, followed by a consistent response, followed by an artificial reward for demonstrating the correct response, called a Discrete Trial. This type of ABA is typically done at the table or a location with increased physical and visual structure. For example, DTT would require a child to say "block" when an adult is holding up a block. As a reward for saying "block" the child would receive a preferred cracker. Naturalistic methods utilize variations of the instruction (that mean the same thing), followed by a consistent response; and then followed by a natural reward pertaining to the instruction or situation. Naturalistic ABA focuses on embedding the skill teaching into the child's natural environment with emphasis on a related reward to the activity or situation. For example, natural ABA would require a child to say "cracker" to obtain a cracker during snack time at the dining room table instead of during a table activity not involving a natural mealtime of the day. When a child when a child struggles with learning a particular skill, a highly-structured teaching method is needed in order for the child to acquire the skill. Utilizing both highly structured and naturalistic methods of ABA common and is a part of the child's individualized program, determined by a trained clinician and the family (Rogers & Dawson, 2009; Cooper et al, 2007).

Now, there are a few different types of ABA; all which utilize the same foundation. Under the ABA umbrella you will find therapies labeled Naturalistic, Early Start Denver Model, Discrete Trial, Verbal Behavior, Pivotal Response Treatment and Precision Teaching. I have found that the Autism Speaks website contains a nice objective description of all of them except for Precision Teaching. Below is a table outlining some of the basic features of the ABA types. I would encourage you to start with one, and determine if it is a good fit for you. The table, and this book, will get you started toward understanding what each type of ABA could look like.

For the purpose of this book, naturalistic, ESDM and discrete trial methods are referenced. I have covered much more detail on ABA therapy in Chapter 5, Family-Centered ABA: Casi's Approach.

Table: Types of ABA Therapy

ABA Type	Session Structure	Target Behaviors	Intensity
Naturalistic or Incidental Teaching	Very natural, play-like setting including activities on the floor and table, utilizing both internal and external rewards. Typically adult directed, but can have child directed activities	All skills taught within a natural routine or environment. Goals are embedded into instruction	25-40 hours is recommended per week. Families are encouraged to use the principals with the child when therapists are not present
Discrete Trial Training (DTT)	Most skills are targeted at the table. External rewards are mostly used. Rapid trials of skill teaching occur	All areas of skill deficit	25-40 per week hours is recommended
Early Start Denver Model (ESDM)	Natural and play based method. Child choice and attention and motivation are hallmarks. Utilizes joint activity routines to teach desired skills	All domains of development are targeted as well as child-adult-peer relationships	20-25 hours per week is desired. Parents and families are to use same principals at home with their child
Verbal Behavior (VB)	A VB program can be utilized on its own, in a designated therapy session. Or it can be used in conjunction with the language portion of another ABA program	Main focus is learning language and helping a child make a connection between a word and its value	30 or more hours per week of scheduled therapy

Sources Used for Table Content: Cooper et al, 2007; Rogers & Dawson, 2009).

Table Continued

ABA Type	Session Structure	Target Behaviors	Intensity
Pivotal Response Training (PRT)	Child directed, motivational strategies, and focus are hallmarks. Pinpointing the child's play activities and skills are crucial	Teaches language, decreases self-stimulatory behaviors, increases social skills and communication	25 or more hours are encouraged. All members of child's family and extended family are encouraged to learn the principles and utilize them in everyday life with the child.
Precision Teaching	Skills are taught with rapid repetition, are timed, and sometimes used in combination with DTT. Skill acquisition and progress are directly related to how effective the teaching methods are	Addresses the curriculum and teaching strategies used with children	Utilized with all teaching methods. No time recommendation.

Sources Used for Table Content: Cooper et al, 2007; Rogers & Dawson, 2009).

- **ABA Teaching Loop**

Casi (Clinician): Let's break down the components of ABA, as outlined above. Whether very structured or very natural versions of ABA are being implemented, there is a common teaching loop that ensues within every teaching opportunity. The very first part of this teaching loop is an instruction or cue to the learner (child). This beginning step can be a verbal instruction given by another person, an environmental cue, or a biological cue. An environmental cue is something in the environment, which triggers a specific behavior, such as a dark room, sunshine, or rain. A biological cue is something within our bodies that trigger us to behave in a certain way, such as hunger, needing to go to the bathroom, or having a headache. These triggers are the first step in teaching a specific action (Cooper et al, 2007).

Next, a response is required in regards to the specific instruction, cue, or trigger. To help a learner achieve the correct response, sometimes a prompt is required. A prompt is simply a way to help the learner demonstrate the correct response to the initial instruction. This can look like physical help or verbal help, such as a therapist putting their hands over the child's hands and helping to show them the desired object, or providing the word "cracker" written on a piece of paper when asking a child what the object is on the table. These prompts can help a learner know what the correct response is, without experiencing too much error. The specific skill being taught determines the level of prompt or support needed for each child. It is important to consult with a behavior therapist when utilizing prompts and supports. The therapist ensures there are ample learning opportunities for the learner, and ensures that prompts are used correctly (Cooper et al, 2007). Now for the last step: the reward!! After the learner demonstrates the correct response (even with the help of a prompt), the therapist provides a reward or reinforcement. In order to teach a new skill/behavior, or change a pre-existing behavior, there needs to be an incentive. It's similar to why adults go to work. Most adults would not go to work if they did not get paid to do so. The same goes for all behavior changes. There needs to be a reward so the learner thinks, "hey, this prize is great to have! I want to get it again." Once this teaching loop is complete, it is repeated multiple times for the same skill across multiple therapy sessions, until the therapist deems the learner has mastered the skill. This is how therapists teach skills to individuals with gaps in their development (Cooper et al, 2007).

Diagram of ABA Teaching Loop

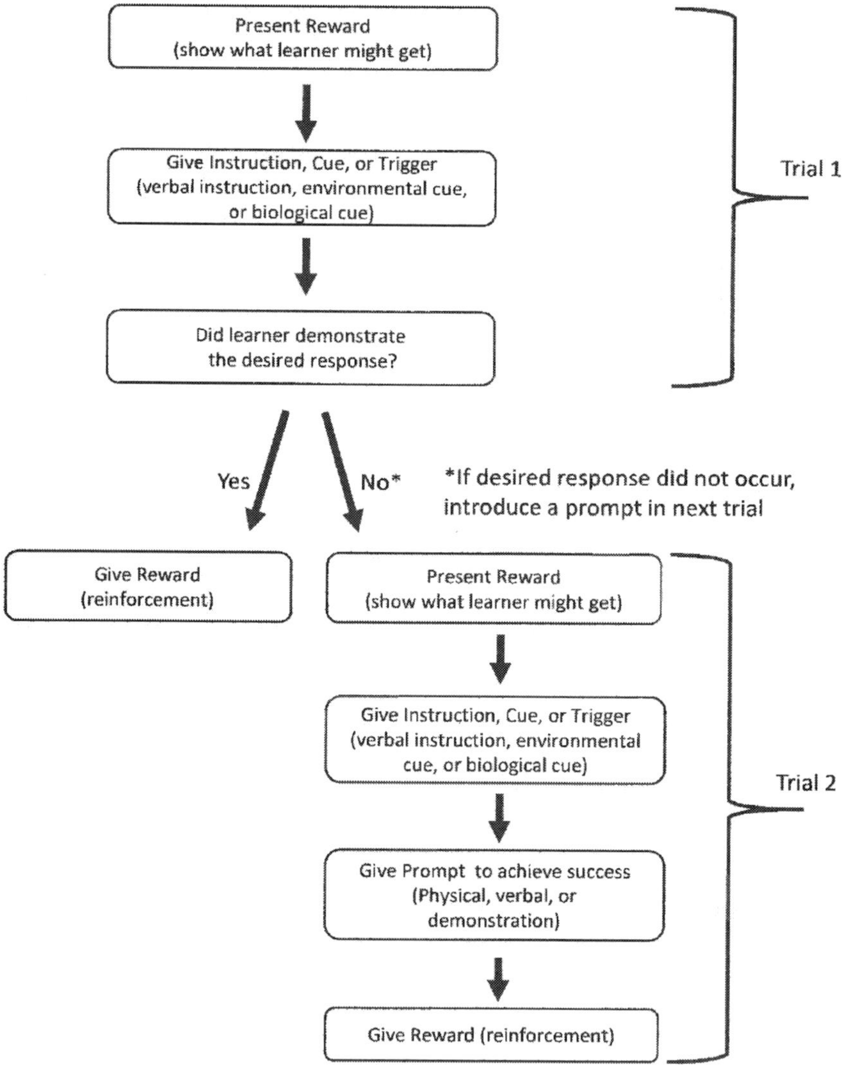

- **Following Through with Consequences (not Punishment)**

Casi (Clinician): There are many basic ABA principles parents are taught during any given therapy session. It can be overwhelming just to hear of a new way to interact with a child; however, it is very helpful to "convert" to a behavior mindset. One of the biggest ABA rules is to follow through with all expectations and demands set for the child. For example, when you ask your child to put their shoes on, don't say it over and over again. Say it one time, then make sure they are doing it. When you give the expectation of "one more bite, then all done," stick with it. Now, when most parents hear this, they say: "Yep, I follow through with most of what I ask him/her to do." I completely understand how difficult it is to follow through all of the time. However, if you do not, you are teaching them to ignore you. You are teaching them that what you say or what you ask of them is not important, and that it is okay if just tune you out (Cooper et al, 2007). While follow-through is a good strategy for all kids, it is especially important for children with autism. The reason is because of their amazing ability to learn behavioral contingencies and expectations very fast...meaning, you only have to not follow through one time and they will establish that this is how it should be every time, that they do not have to listen, and that it is not important. They quickly perceive that you do not mean business.

What if you can't follow through with what you ask? My rule of thumb then is: don't ask. Do not place an expectation on them until you can guarantee that you can follow through. Do not ask them to clean up their toys if you cannot ensure that they actually do it. Make life easier for yourself! Changing a learned behavior of tuning you out or not listening is harder with every moment that you don't follow through. Set expectations and a clear contingency is how they navigate each environment with each person.

- **Redirecting a Child (Redirect)**

Casi (Clinician): What does it mean to "redirect" a child? This means that when they want one thing, or are behaving in a way that is undesirable, you "direct" them to something else. For example, if a child wants a piece of candy in a grocery store and they are continuously saying "I want candy," you say "No, you cannot have candy." Then, you redirect the child by pointing out other interesting things in the store that will take their attention away from the coveted candy.

- **Skill of Generalization**

Casi (Clinician): Another huge component of an ABA is to see if the child will demonstrate the same skills in an artificial environment. This is called generalization. For an individual with autism, generalization is difficult because it requires the ability to change behavior in an environment, based on situational and social cues. The individual needs to be able to see a similar situation with familiar components, and know that a specific behavior is expected. The reason this is difficult for a child with ASD is because the way they process environmental cues is to "take a picture" of the situation's components and memorize them so when those components are put together again, they know what to do. If only one or two or some of the components are there, and not all of them, the "picture" is not retrieved from memory and therefore the child does not know what is expected of them. Specific work needs to be done in an intervention program to promote generalization abilities. This is done through many different people and situations where the skill is targeted with facilitation. For example, if the goal was to have the child ask for something he/she wants by using "I want ____", they would need to ask with Mom and Dad and their teacher at school - possibly with Grandma or aunts and uncles. Further, they would need to ask for a variety of objects/activities. This lets the child know that they need to use this skill with all people in all environments.

- **Hallmarks of Development**

Casi (Clinician): Along with the two concepts mentioned above, the ability to imitate is essential to early development. If a child does not see the value in mimicking what others do, they will not learn the same skills as other children. Imitation is how we learn as infants and children. Whether it is speech, motor movements, facial expressions or gestures, imitating another person's actions is how we learn important behavioral contingencies (i.e., I act a certain way and get a specific response or reward) (Cooper et al, 2007; Rogers & Dawson, 2009).

In order to better understand the areas your child currently or potentially will find challenging, it is important to have a basic understanding of early development. One of the hallmarks is shared enjoyment and joint attention. Shared enjoyment is where your child and either you or another person will both look like they are enjoying the same activity or object because of the same reasons (i.e., it's funny, it is interesting, or it is fun to play with). Joint attention can be related to shared enjoyment; however, it is slightly different. Joint attention is where both your child and their play partner are both attending to an object at the same time. In order to be socially aware of another person and learn from them in an environment, a child has to contain the ability to attend jointly and share enjoyment with another person (Rogers & Dawson, 2009).

- **Theory of Mind**

Casi (Clinician): The theory of mind deficit in children with autism is a huge reason why these individuals appear to be self-centered, inflexible and lacking in the ability to think about others. The reality is that they just do not have the ability to see another person's point of view. They cannot "put themselves in another person's shoes," or see a situation in any other way than their own. They truly believe that everyone thinks like them and therefore they do not understand why another person should be consulted about any part of their life. What they want should make sense, and everyone obviously should comply (Cooper et al, 2007; Rogers & Dawson, 2009).

Although they may lack this ability innately, it is teachable. To develop this ability and create understanding around the fact that other people don't always think like they do, they must practice! During activities where the child is pushed out of their comfort zone and made to accept another person's ideas, you can help them cope. Help them calm down by deep breathing, and give them an end point to their discomfort. What I mean is: add structure by saying something like "first we do it my way, then we do it your way." This added structure will help them understand that it is not always someone else's choice, but sometimes it is; and there is an end point. Then their understanding will increase and a learning opportunity is there.

- **Use a Curriculum and Set Goals**

Casi (Clinician): The curriculum that I like to use includes all developmental domains: expressive and receptive language, play, imitation, joint attention, fine and gross motor skills, behavior, social interaction with adults and with peers, and parent goals. Then, as the clinician, I can determine where there are gaps in the child's development and we can work on those holes. It also gives the parent a comprehensive look at areas where their child is struggling the most, and why. And, how these areas of struggle compare to same-age peers.

Carrie (Mother): After several ABA therapy sessions with Casi, she presented us with Daniel's first "Goals List". It contained goals she felt were appropriate with Daniel, based on her observations in the sessions. I found the goals to be very tangible, and also very remedial. The goals helped me understand Daniel's developmental delays more clearly. The goals also helped me understand that Casi had a plan for helping him reach the goals. However, I did not understand exactly how the plan would work. This is what I continued to learn as we moved forward.

In this original set of goals, Casi outlined goals in 6 areas of development. For your reference, I've listed one goal from each development area below.

1. Receptive Language
   Goal: Daniel will respond to yes and no questions.

2. Expressive Language
   Goal: Daniel will 'ask' for help

3. Social Skills
   Goal: Daniel will respond to his name by looking up and making eye contact.

4. Imitation
   Goal: Daniel will imitate one-step motor actions.

5. Play Skills
   Goal: Daniel will use placeholders in play scenarios

6. Emotion Regulation
   Goal: Daniel will wait for the preferred object without getting upset.

- **Splinter Skills**

Casi (Clinician): In autism, there are what is called "splinter skills." This is where a child demonstrates higher level skills, yet they skipped some of the fundamentals and therefore have gaps in their development. Without a developmental curriculum, finding those gaps would be more difficult and possibly would never be filled in (Rogers & Dawson, 2009; Cooper et al, 2007).

What this means is that there are skills that we need to teach the child which come before some skills the child already demonstrates. The reason this happens is because development in children with autism does not follow a natural progression according to development. More often it is based on the child's interests. A lot of the time, the kids who have many splinter skills appear to have more skills than they really do because they are showing higher level abilities, but they still have not mastered the fundamentals. For example, a child with a very large vocabulary may not understand the meaning of the words he/she is saying, or a child who can match colors and shapes because they are interested in those things cannot match identical pictures. This is the reason why having either a good grasp on development or using a developmental curriculum is important - then there are no skills missed!

Chapter Summary

- Applied Behavior Analysis (ABA) is a research based, systematic approach to working with children with autism.
- Within any skill instruction, an ABA teaching loop will be present.
- Following through with consequences is not considered punishment. If you cannot follow through, do not put a demand on a child.
- Redirecting a child is an important strategy to use when it is difficult for them to stop asking or commenting on a particular topic.
- Generalizing a skill means that a child can demonstrate a skill in many different environments with different people.
- Imitation, joint attention, and shared enjoyment are hallmarks of development that are difficult for children with autism.
- The ability to see another's perspective is an essential component to social interaction.
- Creating goals based on a curriculum is recommended when working with children with autism.
- Splinter Skills are indicators of gaps in a child's development.

Chapter 5:
Family-Centered ABA: Casi's Approach

- **Why I Do It This Way**

Casi (Clinician): When I was utilizing ABA in the beginning of my career, I interacted with the parents of my clients a lot. I was in their house for 15-20 hours per week. They got used to seeing me, and, at times, I became "one of the family." During this time, I was not in the role of providing guidance to them, rather my job was to report to them what I was doing, why I was doing it, and what results I was seeing, in the moment, throughout my sessions.

Throughout these day-to-day interactions, I would see the emotions on the parents' faces when either they would have a rough night with their child, or a positive breakthrough at school or in the child's other therapies. I would see their heartbreak when a behavior popped up and they had no strategies or answers to help. I saw their need for guidance, support, knowledge, and compassion when interacting with their service providers. It was that need that ignited me to strive to really try to "get it" as a provider.

What do I mean by "get it," you ask? I mean when a provider/professional really takes the time to listen, process, and put themselves in the parents' shoes to help remedy the situation. This is how I got started in doing things "my way." It is why I decided to pursue a psychology degree and counseling license to go with my field experience of behavior therapy and applied behavior analysis. These tools help me help the family achieve whatever quality of life they are looking for. These tools help me work with parents the on their grief and anxiety surrounding parenting and their child. I make a point to ensure they know I am here for them, for their child, in whatever way, on whatever path they need to take to get to their "big picture goals." My psychology background and counseling license assists me in being able to address the family system, while also targeting the individual goals and skill areas their child needs, which is supported by the amazing training in ABA that I have received. This combination of education and compassion focused on family-centered treatment is "my way" of doing ABA.

What does this look like? For me, it is making sure the parents know that I am here for them. I am there if there is a problem at school, at the library, at the karate studio or even at church! I am always ready to listen and figure out what the best option is for the family. This may require me to attend the karate session, go to church with my clients or do a school observation. I am okay with seeing a family multiple times a week, if it is clinically necessary or financially feasible. Those two qualifiers are the utmost importance. I don't have a set structure that each family must follow. I individualize it depending on the needs of the child and family. At the forefront are the parents or caregivers. They must be involved at each session in some capacity in order to be a part of my caseload. This is "my way" of practicing family-centered care.

Another uniqueness to my therapy approach is that I prefer to have home sessions with my clients and families. When I think of 'getting it," from the parents' perspectives, I think of being in their home, seeing things they see, and working with them to resolve or solve the problems. In my experience, most children act a little different, if not very different, in an office or clinic setting. I see that as a huge barrier to really helping families with the real life concerns they have and face on a daily basis.

From my perspective, interventions that do not have a strong family component are not as effective as they could be. In my experience, children with parents who are highly involved in their children's therapy sessions (i.e., talking to the providers, getting homework to carry over treatment objectives at home, and being a part of therapy sessions on a weekly basis) are children who generalize skills faster and tend to have a higher rate of progress. If this sounds like a good fit, find a provider who can offer this "whole package." This would be a service provider who is able to either help with a variety of concerns, or who can to tell you who to talk to get help. The presence of these characteristics in a service provider could help decrease your stress and anxiety. The overall goal, in my opinion, is to help you become the best parent and provider you can be for your child.

For some ABA-specific service providers, the focus is the child's treatment and the number of hours of one-to-one services the child gets. I believe, however, this is only a portion of the important pieces of helping children. If the parent had support from a service provider to help get extended family on board, (like grandparents, aunts, uncles, or cousins) with the skills and behaviors a child needs to work on to have a better quality of life, it would be the best possible combination and outcome for the child. There are so many parents I have talked to who have thought, over and over, about how to tell family and how to explain what is going on with their child - how to make them realize what they are going through, and therefore how to help everyone succeed. What about schools, childcares, or other service providers? Having them communicate and work together for the benefit of the child is essential to increasing the rate of progress! These are the types of support and resources I believe every family should have access to, if they want it. This is also why I feel so strongly about finding providers who will fit with the family's needs. Finding a speech therapist, occupational therapist, or ABA provider that individualizes every aspect of a child's program and feels like the right fit is the first order of business. Trust your gut instinct; it is seldom wrong!

- **Session Management**

Casi (Clinician): The way I structure my session is to check in with how their past days, weekend or weeks have gone. I ask what kind of positive things are happening and what kinds of things the family wants to work on. Then we dig way deep into these topics to get to some solutions that the family can use until we meet again. Sometimes this requires the parents to look through their own parenting "lens". This could also include some grief work with how they are handling the diagnosis. Each session is different. After we deep dive into the problems, we end with some positives. This helps the family know that there are always things to be thankful for.

- **Simulation of Everyday Challenges**

Casi (Clinician): As stated above I like to be in the home when doing treatment sessions because it is easier and more realistic to simulate the real life challenges my clients' families face. With that being said, a large number of play activities I do with my clients are meant to trigger a larger, more intrusive issue within the family dynamic or the child's everyday life. Using the role play of these challenges, I can get a glimpse of what the family goes through on a daily basis and therefore can offer some tips and assistance for when they come up again.

I have found it very important to remain positive with the families that I have worked with. To me this means that any step in the right direction or any progress should be celebrated. There is some evidence to support the idea that a plateauing effect happens in therapy. This can be very frustrating for both the parent and the clinician. When a plateau effect occurs in skills progression, we will think differently and try new things, think outside the box. In my experience, I have found that stagnation occurring from the materials in a therapy environment can be the culprit. Working with a professional who is open to trying new things and who admits when things are not going right is key to getting over these humps. And after we climb and conquer the hill, we can celebrate whatever amount of progression was made. I also believe in realistic goals. A goal set needs to be attainable for any child and parent. Otherwise, no one experiences success, frustration mounts, positive attitudes diminish, and skill development does not occur and plateaus ensue. Each child has their own celebrations and challenges, and those should be addressed in an individualized way. In my opinion, professionals should be open to that.

Chapter 6:
Family-Centered ABA Therapy: A Mom's Lessons

- **My Lessons Learned as a Parent of a Newly-Diagnosed Child**

Carrie (Mother): There are several life-changing lessons Jake and I learned through our experience in ABA therapy with Casi. These lessons completely transformed my approach to parenting. I am a much better mother because Casi coached Jake and me as parents in addition to working with Daniel.

As first-time parents, we were still figuring out how just to be parents. With the diagnosis as a reality, we had to increase our awareness of what Daniel needed from us and how we could help him. Casi's therapeutic approach involves the entire family. She works to engage each family member in the effort of helping the child with ASD, teaching many important ABA concepts and lessons to help the whole family. I've shared many of these concepts and lessons in this chapter.

When I first heard about ABA (Applied Behavior Analysis), I had zero understanding of how behavioral therapy might be administered. I did not know what to expect, but I was very interested in starting. I did not want Daniel to lose more time without intervention.

One thing I learned early on from either some of my reading or in our early therapies is that imitation and eye contact are essential in order for a typical child to learn. With Daniel having deficiencies in both of these areas, his developmental progress would be severely slowed down compared to a typical child. So, how could we help him gain eye contact and imitation skills?

My view is that autism strips a child of natural learning capabilities. There are some atypical tendencies evident in a lot of children on the spectrum. These tendencies put up barriers to learning. For example, why is it that many children on the spectrum do not seem to have the natural instinct of using words to communicate? Why is it that many are not motivated by social interaction, but would rather self-isolate? These tendencies can make it more difficult for children to learn and pick up new skills, even if they have the cognitive capabilities to learn.

The actual process of learning is a skill that they need to be taught. It is possible for them to learn how to learn! Behavioral therapy recognizes this fact. As a parent, this was an incredibly enlightening concept. Children on the spectrum won't just learn basic skills without intervention, like typical children do. You have to teach them how to learn.

- **Lesson 1: Life Will Be Easier for You if You Use Your Words**

Carrie (Mother): A main lesson we learned from Casi is that we had to teach Daniel "life will be easier for you if you use your words." In our ABA sessions, Casi helped us understand that Daniel did not have natural tendencies to use words to communicate. His natural tendencies to communicate or get his needs met were driven by other instincts, such as throwing a tantrum, or hitting, or pulling you toward what he wanted and putting your hand on it. An early approach that Casi taught was that we had to stop "reading his mind". We had to demand more from him in terms of communication. We wanted words from him because he actually could speak. He was just unaware of how powerful those words were and therefore did not know he needed to use them.

- **Lesson 2: My Expectations of Daniel Were Too Low**

Carrie (Mother): As we moved through the ABA therapy sessions, Daniel would begin making some progress in his behavior; but then we might have a few harder days. We began to notice this pattern before he would make new breakthroughs.

When you are working diligently to help your child learn new skills, and then you see them make progress, and you think: "Sweet! We are past those harder days." Then, the old behaviors return, and you think: "Wait, why isn't he still moving forward?" It's discouraging. That's where the follow through and patience is so important - because in two or three days, your child may make a giant leap forward in a separate skill, and those others that regressed could come right back. And you can look back and say: "Oh, now I see what was going on when he had a couple of hard days! He was trying to make room for a new skill!" But if you give up during those hard days and don't keep up with the therapies, follow through, and tactics, you can delay the positive progress.

The learning cycle is another item that is counter-intuitive to me, as someone untrained in early childhood development. This learning cycle enlightened me, and it made the tougher days with Daniel a bit more optimistic because Jake and I could say: "I wonder what new leap he's getting ready for?" It helped us welcome the harder days a bit more because we knew they actually might mean he was progressing. Again, this was initially very counter-intuitive to me.

Daniel would give a final big burst of "holding out" or would resist conforming. Then it's like he realized: "Okay … this is how it's going to be. I need to keep doing this skill." And, then he'd turn the corner permanently. It's awesome to observe this transition, but highly taxing on your endurance. Without a trained ABA therapist at hand, I know that I would not have known how far to push Daniel in expecting a certain skill. I would not have known what was reasonable or unreasonable. I would have not trusted my own judgment. I would have lacked confidence. My expectations of Daniel would have been too low. Casi helped us see Daniel's potential. She guided us to places that we could not take either ourselves or Daniel.

Jake and I truly felt that Casi was Daniel's biggest fan and best cheerleader. Because she is so well-trained and knowledgeable about early childhood development, she often had higher expectations of Daniel than Jake or I did. I would often think, "Do you really think he can learn that?" when she would introduce a new goal for Daniel. And she was so optimistic about what he could learn. It was comforting and encouraging to have her want to push Daniel into new and higher levels of learning. There were several times throughout our therapy where I might have settled and been happy with the progress to date, without expecting a lot more. Find a therapist who believes in your child's ability to make forward progress!

- **Lesson 3: We Replaced "Punishment" with Behavioral Strategies**

Carrie (Mother): When Daniel started biting and hitting family members and friends at about 16-17 months of age, we would give him a timeout. That's just what you do as a parent, right? The child is supposed to be upset because you are removing them from friends or toys. For Daniel, timeouts were not effective in resolving the aggression situation. The biting and hitting continued even though we were giving timeouts. Why didn't he care about getting a timeout? Shouldn't he care about being in "trouble"?

I was very anxious about his biting behavior, and I wanted it to end. I have to admit I was self-conscious as a parent because I knew other parents would look at the biting as a reflection of Jake and me as "bad" parents. I did not know why Daniel was biting and hitting.

Casi taught us that Daniel's biting and hitting was not out of anger towards us or other children, but about getting his needs met. With Daniel experiencing a speech delay (along with expressive and receptive communication delays), he did not have any other recourse except to bite, hit, or walk away from a situation he didn't like. He didn't know how to say "No". He didn't know how to say "I don't want that". He did not know how to say "Move" or "Go Away" or "Stop it". So what else could he do in the absence of civil communication? Answer: "Fight or Flight". And, a lot of times he chose "fight".

We had to ratchet down our own anger response to his biting and hitting. I believe it is human nature to get angry and defensive when someone bites you or hits you. Casi taught us how to control our own emotions and understand that Daniel's biting was simply a behavior we needed to confront very calmly and methodically, without anger and without typical punishments for this "bad behavior". He was not being naughty when he bit or hit. He was trying to navigate his environment. Casi helped us see his aggression for what it really was.

Casi helped us understand that Daniel often bit when he became overwhelmed with a particular person or situation. He would lash out in order to get that uncomfortable situation to end. Receiving a timeout because of the biting gave him quiet time. The timeout truly gave him an "out" from the challenging situation of dealing with friends or parents and whatever demand we were placing on him. Time alone or an escape from his surroundings was what he craved. We quickly abolished timeouts from our home after we learned more about Daniel's challenges and motivators.

We began our entrance into behavioral strategies with a new perspective on what it meant to punish or discipline a child. We started learning about behavioral strategies that would help Daniel tolerate and navigate uncomfortable situations like sharing a toy, having another child yelling too close to him, getting carried by Jake or me to a place he didn't want to go, or encouraging him to persevere in challenging situations.

- **Lesson 4: We Had to Learn the Term "Behavioral Strategies" (Motivations and Rewards)**

Carrie (Mother): Along with eliminating any intent to punish Daniel, we had to replace punishment and anger with behavioral strategies. This was a hard lesson for me to learn in that I did not really understand a child's motivations or what could serve as a proper reward. The best way I can describe it is to say that behavioral strategies are all about motivations and rewards. That is what Casi taught us. I would encourage you to answer these questions about your child.

- What is your child's favorite toy?
- What do they like to play with the most?
- What are your child's favorite foods or desserts?
- What are your child's favorite places to go?
- What makes your child laugh or smile?
- Who are your child's favorite people to be around?
- Does your child have a favorite game? Or a favorite song?
- Does your child like stickers or stamps?
- Who are your child's favorite cartoon, movie, or book characters?

Once you can answer the above questions and other similar questions, you can start using that information to communicate with your child in a more meaningful way. You will be on your way to eliminating an attitude of punishment for your child and moving into a world of thoughtful, methodical behavioral strategy in partnership with your child.

- **Lesson 5: You Cannot Skip Steps in the Developmental Process (Splinter Skills)**

Carrie (Mother): I've become fascinated with the information around developmental progression for early childhood development. Before working with Casi, I never really understood, that there are mandatory steps or milestones a child must master in order to appropriately move to the next milestone. The brain does not allow for an effective way of skipping the order. Casi was very good at identifying when Daniel had developed some splinter skills and left other skills behind. We would have to focus on those lagging areas and help him round out his development. She used a consistent curriculum with Daniel, with all the developmental mastery areas listed out. On the curriculum hard copy, she would use yellow highlighter on each skill that Daniel mastered. That way, it was very easy to see how much Daniel was accomplishing, or still lacked, for each curriculum level. Casi was very disciplined in not allowing Daniel's splinter skills to run away before doing the harder work to catch him up on the skills he had more difficulty learning.

In my own mind, I view splinter skills as in the images below. Imagine that the circle contains all the skills needed for early childhood development. With splinter skills, the child may be advancing greatly with a particular skill set in one direction, but leaves other skills unimproved. This would be the first circle. As you start "rounding out" the skill set by focus and practice on skill mastery through ABA therapies, the skills "left behind" or splintered can start catching up (middle circle) so that you move as close to the well-rounded skill set (full circle) as possible. This is just how I think about splinter skills and the need for addressing them.

"Many Splinter Skills"
Conceptual illustration of severe areas of delay

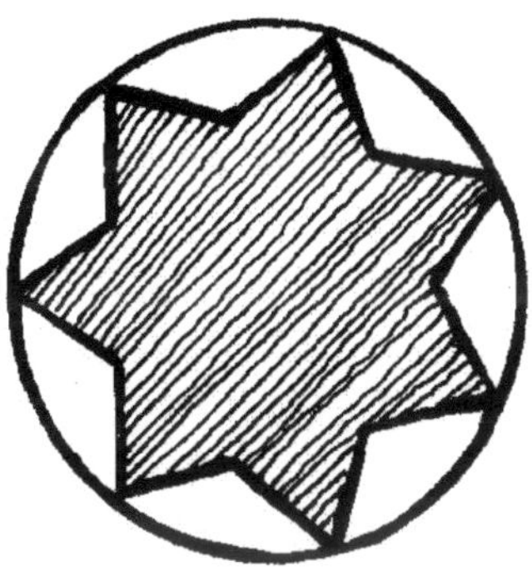

"Some Splinter Skills"
Conceptual illustration of remaining gaps, but are skills are rounding out

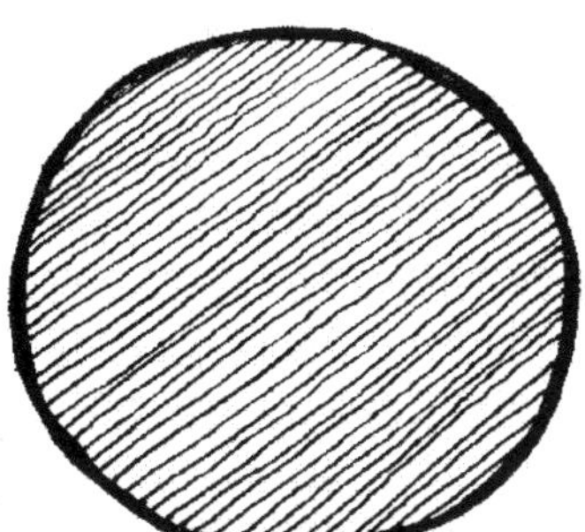

"No Splinter Skills"
Conceptual illustration of gaps all filled in

- **Lesson 6: The "Theory of Mind" is a Powerful Communication Barrier.**

Carrie (Mother): Casi explained to us that there is a "theory of mind" deficit that often displays in children on the spectrum. Basically, it is difficult for them to understand that another person may have a different perspective than they do. Because it makes sense for them to like or dislike something, the child does not know to recognize that another person may feel differently than they do. The ASD child does not feel they need to ask because it already makes sense to them, in their own way. Therefore, it should make the same sense to another person. The discussion isn't necessary. Their view is simply the reality of the situation.

To address this deficit, we practiced playing many different board games in our ABA sessions. Focus areas of game playing included taking turns and finishing the game before Daniel decided he was done playing. We were trying to stretch out his attention span and the length of time he could do something that was not highly preferred. When it was clear he wanted to finish the game immediately, we practiced taking "one more turn" before finishing.

In other instances, we had to practice coping with him being very competitive. He would always want to win, but sometimes he wouldn't. So we had to help him work through those emotions.

Another basic thing we practiced in playing games was actually just how to set up the environment for playing a game. A basic aspect of starting a board game is to pick your player. Who do you want to be for the game? What color will you be? What color will your playmates be? This sounds simple, but this is an actual skill that Daniel needed to learn. How do you negotiate who will be what player? How do you decide who will go first in the game? How do you decide how long you will play?

All of these things were important "practicing" aspects of game play that we walked through in ABA sessions. For example, if we were setting up the game and picking the color of the players we were all going to be, we would ask Daniel to hand out the players. Daniel would often pick the color he wanted first; for example, the blue player. And then he would give Casi the red player. He would decide for her that she would have red. But what if Casi didn't want the red player? What if she wanted the yellow one or, heaven forbid, the blue one that Daniel had already picked?

This is a real-life situation that Daniel will face with other children. Casi worked to teach Daniel how to offer her the remaining colors of the players (yellow, red, green, for example), rather than "forcing" his choice (the red one) on her. So, Casi would teach Daniel how to offer the remaining colors and he would practice letting her pick her color. We went through this exercise many, many times.

So, in the game, if Daniel wanted the blue player, then it should be fine with everyone else for him to pick blue. If he wanted juice, then everyone else should want juice too. If he was done playing the game, everyone else should be done, too. Casi worked with Daniel to help him see another person's perspective. She focused on teaching Daniel how to ask questions of the other person he's interacting with. She taught him to offer choices of toys and practiced asking another playmate to play with him. She helped him soften his approach in playing with other playmates. She gave us tactics for giving him new words to relate to others in a way that would be more socially appropriate.

- **Lesson 7: Learning How An "Extinction Burst" Completes the Meltdown Cycle**

Carrie (Mother): An extinction burst episode might start in an ABA session when asking the child to clean up, or telling him to put the train in the bin before playing with the beans; but the child will not do so. The child doesn't want to clean up. I exaggerate a little, but when you or the ABA therapist pushes this type of "button" or "trigger point," it's as though you have asked the two-year-old child to go against a long-held principle for which he's prepared to fight to the death. But this is what you need to do. You need to trip these triggers and push through their fallout.

With ABA, I feel it is a continuous "stretching" process, taking the child out of their typical comfort zone. Some of the ABA techniques Casi employed required Daniel to expand his coping skills and persist through uncomfortable moments and minutes where he would have preferred to indulge in his comfort-seeking tendencies. One example is a play date where he didn't want to take turns. Daniel might have a meltdown and run to his room. We would go get him and bring him back into the situation of turn-taking with the other child. The other child might have to sit and wait 10-20 minutes for Daniel to work through the extinction burst cycle before he would be ready to take that next step of completing the sharing or turn-taking process.

It's like a very long timeout from your day, where you have to remember: "What was I asking him to do right before his meltdown? Give up the toy to the friend. Okay, when he's done crying and settles down, he will still need to give the toy to the friend." Time stops until he gives the toy to the friend. You do not move on with your day or any other activity until the follow through on the request is complete.

Unless you are comfortable with this concept of an indefinite "stop" in the moment with your child, then the follow through is nearly impossible to administer because the child truly may seem inconsolable. But he is not: you can console him. You just have to help him push beyond his natural tendencies to fight the desired, appropriate social behavior. And, in doing so, you are starting to give him tools to console himself, to self-regulate his emotions, to make new choices, and to have more appropriate responses to his environment.

For "untrained" parents, it seems like there is no end in sight to these moments of meltdown. What if you are in the grocery store? What if you are in a parking lot? What if you are running late to an important appointment? There are times where you just simply can't conduct an ABA session event. You cannot take the time required for perfect follow through.

That's why you can purposefully "set the stage" for a meltdown or "trigger" a child's sensitivity in the context of an ABA session, in order to simulate the difficult moments you might encounter in real life. In the ABA sessions, once you see the extinction burst process a couple of times, you can see that there truly is a pattern to the response of the child, and that the child makes such a big achievement upon following through (or complying) with the request made of them. Those are such proud moments for me as a parent to have arrived at; like summiting a mountain!

It's invigorating o see your child move past something that had been so difficult for him, where he didn't understand what was being required or why. He's confused and tries all that he knows has helped him before (biting, hitting, running away, hitting himself, crying, trying to do a different activity), but those are not good options in the real world ... and then it's like a light bulb goes on, when the child realizes that the only other thing he can do is what is being asked of him...and then he does it! If they did it once, they can do it again, and then practice again and again.

What was amazing to see through the course of our ABA sessions with Daniel is that the extinction burst cycle started out very long (like 20 minutes), but then continued to get shorter and shorter...until Daniel just started learning to follow directions. It was truly amazing to me to see this process happen in my child. He was gaining tools to interact with his environment; tools he would not have been able to find on his own, like a typical child can. As hard as it was to watch him go through this process, seeing him gain life skills was literally life-changing for us and for him.

During the early ABA sessions, when Daniel was still displaying heavy reliance on his old strategies for coping (hitting and biting to escape certain situations), it was hard to watch him stretch to learn new skills. You see your sweet boy being confused and angry and crying and fighting. You are testing his will with this new level of follow through on requests. It's like you have to become numb to major offenses such as getting bitten without pulling back, getting hit and not being able to flinch, and not responding when you see your baby hit himself. Have faith that the biting and the hitting will stop once he realizes he needs to try something new. You have to remain calm and unresponsive even while your baby looks at you with confusion and anger, and feels misunderstood. You simply make the same request ("Put the train in the basket."). Then, (after one or 20 minutes) you'll see your child get to a point of exasperation and exhaustion and compromise where he successfully pushes through his own barrier of wills. And then comes the awesome moment when the crying stops, he takes deep breaths, and he puts the offending train in the basket. Good job! I knew you could do it! Now, let's play with the beans.

- **Lesson 8: Play Dates Can Be Strategic for Building Communication Skills**

Carrie (Mother): One of the things within my control as Daniel's mom is to help him interact with other children. As we discuss in Chapter 7, Establishing an ABA Home Program, you can make a play date very strategic. Casi taught us how to facilitate a play date so that Daniel could gain skills and build relationships with his peers as part of the experience. This tool is invaluable, and I use it as often as I can

- **Lesson 9: My Child May Struggle with Anxiety, OCD, or Depression**

Casi taught me that children with autism grow up to be adults who struggle with anxiety, obsessive-compulsive disorder (OCD), and depression. This knowledge reinforced my resolve to help Daniel learn self-regulation, healthy coping mechanisms, flexibility, and generalization at as early an age as possible.

One thing I love about the ABA therapy Daniel received was that Casi purposefully, knowledgably, and logically addressed Daniel's anxieties. Some examples of his anxiety and rigidity were regarding his shoes (preferring only one pair), his food (loss of wholeness), and toys (surrounding strong preferences and the loss of perfection). Casi never forced Daniel to do anything. She made requests of him that he didn't like, but she never traumatized him. She dealt with his fears, anxieties, and rigidity in a very respectful and optimistic way.

She showed Jake and me a progressive process that fascinates me. How can you wean your child from a habit, toy, food, or preference that seems so rooted in the core of their being? You can! You can do it respectfully and methodically, but not forcefully. This respectful aspect of Casi's work with Daniel helped me trust her and put my protective instincts at ease.

Whenever we see Daniel tightening up in certain areas, we are prepared to reapply particular ABA techniques so that Daniel can increase his comfort level with things that may not go his way or according to plan. My hope is that he becomes as well adjusted as possible to the world, using a variety of techniques that can bring him more comfort.

- **Lesson 10: My Child Is Not the Only Special Needs or Special Child. Other Children are Special, Too.**

In the early years after you receive the diagnosis, it is easy to feel isolated. It is easy to compare your child to other typical children. It is easy to feel as though your struggle as a special needs parent is particular to you, and that your child is somehow set apart from others…because a lot of times, they are. As part of this process, you may also receive "special treatment" in certain cases. This special treatment enables you to feel as though you might need to get special consideration for particular activities, or special compassion when your child is "misbehaving" or simply in general. It is a nuance of being a special needs family.

One thing I've become enlightened about is that my child is not the only "special" child. Every child is special. And, every child, typical or developmentally delayed, will have challenges specific to them. It would be incorrect for me to look at a family of a typical child, and think they have no major challenges. Their challenges are just different from mine, so they are harder to spot.

Through a variety of scenarios, I've learned that our struggle with autism, while difficult, does not automatically trump situations other families are facing. Autism just happens to be one of our family's challenges.

Daniel is special, but other children are special too. I can have compassion with other children, even if my child sometimes is getting the short end of the stick in particular situations. My child does not always have to win. My goal is to help him navigate through everyday situations and even more challenging situations.

For example, once I had taken Daniel and Caleb to a trampoline center. The boys were playing, and began playing an impromptu game of dodgeball with a couple other kids. There was one boy there who was a couple years older than Daniel and was quite a bit bigger. He also had a very strong throwing arm. Essentially, he "pegged" Daniel a couple of times pretty hard. And, I was starting to get defensive of Daniel. I told the staff member nearby that the larger boy was being kind of rough.

He was like “Yeah, I know. His dad brings him here to burn off energy. I think he might have autism”. And I said defensively, “Well, mine does, too”. The staff worker turned to me with a perplexed look; and then I felt ridiculous like I was starting to play a battle of “whose autism is worse?”

This same staff member pulled the boy aside and challenged him to start throwing the ball toward a basketball hoop quite a ways away. So, he really had to throw it hard to hit the backboard. And the boy was successfully redirected, and he started throwing balls very accurately at the hoop. I was impressed with the way this staff member redirected this other boy. And I felt convicted for my original defensiveness. The defensiveness melted, and I began feeling compassion for this older boy and the dad who brought his boy to burn off energy. The dad was just trying to make it through, and do the best he knew how to do. I get it. My child is not the only special one.

Chapter Summary:

- In our ABA sessions, Casi helped us understand that Daniel did not have natural tendencies to use words to communicate.
- Casi helped us see Daniel's potential. She guided us to places that we could not take ourselves or Daniel.
- As we began working with Casi, she helped us understand that Daniel often bit or hit others when he became overwhelmed with a particular person or situation. He would lash out in order to get that uncomfortable situation to end.
- Behavioral strategies are all about motivations and rewards.
- When splinter skills are present, the child may be advancing greatly with a particular skill set in one direction, but leaving other skills unimproved.
- The theory of mind deficit in children with autism is a huge contributor as to why these individuals seem self- centered, inflexible, and lacking in the ability to think about others. The reality is that they just do not have the ability to see another person's point of view.
- You can purposefully "set the stage" for a meltdown or "trigger" a sensitivity of the child in an ABA session in order to simulate the difficult moments you might encounter in real life.
- Strategic play dates are an effective way of building stronger communication skills and help build relationships with classmates.
- Whenever I see Daniel tightening up in certain areas, we are prepared to reapply particular ABA techniques so that he can increase his comfort level with things that may not go his way or according to plan.

Chapter 7:
Establishing an ABA Home Program

- **What is an ABA Home Program?**

Casi (Clinician): When looking at what services to try with your child, I would highly recommend Applied Behavior Analysis (ABA). This is a treatment method, which is heavily supported by research due to the effectiveness of its methods in teaching children with autism.

Three main components to an ABA Home Program include:

- Goals for the Child
- Curriculum to follow
- Parent Involvement

Within a home program, the clinician establishes goals for the child. The child's therapy "team" targets these goals in a systematic way.

The child's team, in my opinion, consists of the parents, the lead clinician, ABA home therapists, speech therapists, occupational therapists, teachers and any other person who spends a good deal of time with the child. The child's team determines the number of hours each child needs. The frequency and duration of treatment hours are individualized for each child. A family's financial situation, time constraints, and place in the grieving process all play a role in determining what a child's treatment progression will look like. There is no wrong answer.

One component of a sound, effective, successful home program is parental involvement. From my perspective, having a child component, a parent component, and a team component in any intervention is the key to long-term, generalized success. It is my philosophy that the entire family system needs to be addressed in conjunction with individualized child treatment. If this is desired, a family could find a provider that asks to have reoccurring parent meetings, as well as team meetings, if other services providers are involved in treating their child. Furthermore, meetings and check-ins could happen with the family (all members of the family) so that family and parental goals can be created and followed up on as well as addressing any challenging behaviors or skill development updates between and among all environments.

Another essential component to a successful program is communication. At the start of every treatment session, I ask the parents: “So, what has been going on since our last session?” Sometimes parents are forthcoming right away, and sometimes it takes them a while to open up about what really has happened over the last few days. That is ok. It takes time to feel comfortable being open about true struggles and low points. However, if open communication is not present, how can I help? If a child has a perfect day with no behaviors while I am in the home, great; but then how can I help with the hard stuff?

Along with ongoing, open communication, the number of hours spent with the family (all members) is a huge part of a well-rounded treatment program. The times where I have seen the most progress happen are when I am involved with the family; more so than for one-to-one child treatment. My goal is to spend as much time as possible with the child and family combined; so when challenges arise, I can provide direction that is 100% tailored to the family system. What, exactly, does this mean? Well, it means that when I give suggestions, they will be given with the specific family's situation, dynamics, and makeup in mind. There are so many times I hear families say, “Well, he/she told me to do this, but they just don't get our family.” I want to eliminate that saying from every parent's speech! Do they have extra resources? Do they have family support? Are they able to take off work? What level of involvement can they realistically do? These are just a few of the questions I ask myself before making a suggestion or giving a direction I would like them to follow. Without the full comprehension of my client's family life, I feel I am not able to provide them with the best possible service.

Carrie (Mother): In ABA efforts, you can set up a “home program” which can include other people, supervised by your ABA Home Program Supervisor. The cost of therapy can be very daunting. Trying to understand and get insurance coverage is another hurdle. When I learned that we could have some creativity around how we established an ABA program for Daniel, it was refreshing because it meant our money could stretch further and that I could be a stronger influence in my son's progress.

What was amazing to me when we first started learning about ABA was that home programs can have "understudies," or people who get trained by the supervising consultant. I'm going to call these lay people "sub-consultants". The training comes from the ABA therapist who supervises the home program. Casi, with her Master's degree in Clinical Psychology, qualifies as a "supervisor", or lead clinician, for our home program. This program can supplement the primary ABA sessions for ABA therapy whether or not you are conducting your primary ABA sessions in a clinic or at home.

Jake and I were trying to learn as much as we could about the behavioral responses that would help Daniel. Once we learned that ABA can extend beyond the actual therapist, it opened up a lot of options. It also took some pressure off of us to have to fill in all of the gaps on our own. Remember: 25 hours was the goal stated by the clinical psychologist at our diagnosis regarding the desired weekly hours of therapy (if you cannot give "every waking hour"). We were currently at 1.5 hours per week of ABA therapy with Casi. We had about 3 additional hours of therapy going on through the Birth to 3 program. So, we still had a ways to go toward the goal of 25 hours per week of therapy.

- **We Started ABA in the Clinic Setting. Jacob Took the Lead.**

Jacob (Father): I was fortunate to have the freedom to give my son much of the attention he needed. At the time of the diagnosis, Carrie and I were both working full-time. Carrie was working at a marketing agency in Seattle, and I worked for my dad at his construction company.

My parents' support was profoundly important in our early and evolving walk on this journey. They provided their encouragement, help, and acceptance of what we were going through. Because of their support, I reconfigured my workweek to four days instead of five. This allowed me to accommodate one day each week for scheduling our various therapy sessions. Carrie joined me or took lead once per month on this Monday routine.

Carrie (Mother): After about 3 months of ABA therapy in the clinic setting, I started trying to find people who could participate in our home program, as we wanted to get extra hours in for therapy. This was also the point in time when Casi developed Daniel's first round of official ABA goals, so there was a nice reference to use for training the sub-consultants.

Who are the candidates for additional "sub-consultants"? Answer: Just regular people, who can be trained to provide ABA therapy to your child. These people can be other moms, friends, teachers, nannies, babysitters, and you! Really, it's anyone who is coachable, likes your child, and wants to earn some extra money.

Here are some people whom Casi more formally trained for our home program: a mother of a boy on the spectrum, an elementary school teacher who goes to our church, my mother-in-law, and our nanny. What I learned through this effort was that nannies and teachers might actually want to gain these skills, as it can build their career skillset. In addition, you might want to consider giving your nanny a raise if you are adding this additional expectation to your nanny's duties.

"Coach-ability" is perhaps the biggest factor in successful training. Look for people who are willing to take instruction from your ABA supervisor, not people who want to act like the ABA supervisor. You are trying to find people who will guide your child consistently with the ABA supervisor.

Casi (Clinician): One of the major benefits of having a home ABA program is that the child receives a higher frequency of intervention services, at a cost per hour that is lower than that of the program manager or supervisor. These are what Carrie referred to as "sub-consultants." A supervisor is responsible for creating the goals and objectives for the specific child as well as training the "sub-consultants" in executing goals with the child. This method can be more cost effective if the child needs, or parents want, more hours of therapy time per week. This model also requires people coming and going from the house, so for some parents this is not an ideal situation because of their comfort level with people always being in their home. There is also the added stress of finding a person who could be a "sub-consultant," interviewing them, and ensuring they are a 'good fit' with your family.

Carrie (Mother): Before moving on, I have three additional thoughts about what Casi just mentioned. First, I see the increased frequency of services from a variety of individuals as a major "pro" because ABA therapy tries to help the child "generalize" their behavior in different situations. If your child can master skills with different instructors, then it shows that your child is making great progress toward generalization.

Second, you may be uncomfortable having multiple people in your home through the ABA home program. However, it may also be a relief to have people come to you. If you have other children, or it's difficult to organize yourself and get your child out the door to an appointment, then having people come to you can be an amazing reduction of your burden. Put on some coffee and observe a session in your own home. After I had our second child, Caleb, and was on maternity leave, it was wonderful to have Casi or another sub-consultant come to our home. I could care for baby Caleb and observe the ABA session in the comfort of our home.

Third, please make sure you note that ABA home therapy is not just expensive babysitting. It is best if you can stay and observe the session. It was never part of our agreement with Casi that she would watch Daniel independently. We were always present for Casi's sessions. She works with the child and the parents simultaneously. However, when you establish a home program, you may be able to form enough trust in the training of your sub-consultants that they are able to work independently with your child (and give you a break). This needs to be an official discussion and acknowledgement between you and the sub-consultants.

We reached this agreement with two of our sub-consultants: the mother of the boy on the spectrum and our nanny. The mother sub-consultant actually had an amazing therapy room set up in her own home, so I was able to take Daniel to her house for his sessions with her. Sometimes I stayed for the whole session. A lot of times I did not. She had a huge assortment of therapy and engagement tools, including a gymnastics mat and lots of games. It was a better use of her skill set and investments to have Daniel work at her house. As for our nanny, she also worked independently with Daniel. We asked her to incorporate a few key items related to the ABA therapies into Daniel's day, along with filling out data sheets.

- **How We Set Up an ABA Home Program**

The following tables represent the progression of services we had in place for Daniel for certain periods of time. The first 2 years after Daniel's diagnosis were the most intense periods of therapy coordination and delivery. After 2 years of very routine ABA therapy, Casi coached us on phasing out some of the ABA sessions from Casi and our sub-consultants.

- **Daniel: 28 Months (Diagnosis) – 32 Months:**

Before Daniel was 3 years old, while Casi was still working for a local Autism Clinic in the Northwest (Services: ABA Therapy with Casi, Birth to 3 Services)

Session Type	Hours	Therapist/ Consultant	Cost
ABA Therapy: Autism Clinic	1.5	Casi Olson	$120 ($80/hour) Partially covered by insurance
Speech Therapy: Local Early Intervention Agency	2 (2 sessions per week)	Speech Therapist	Subsidized by insurance and other sources
Occupational Therapy: Local Early Intervention Agency	2 (2 sessions per week)	Occupational Therapist	Subsidized by insurance and other sources
Chiropractor	1 (2 sessions per week)	Chiropractor	Paid lump sum for specific amount of sessions
Childcare Center (4 days per week)	~30 hours	Childcare provider	$1700/month
Total per week	**5.5 hours beyond Childcare and Chiropractor**		

Daniel: 32 Months – 3 Years Old:
Services included ABA Therapy (beginning ABA Home Program), Early Intervention Services, and Chiropractor Sessions

Session Type	Hours	Therapist/ Consultant	Cost
ABA Therapy: Autism Clinic	1.5	Casi Olson	$120 ($80/hour)
ABA Therapy: Saturdays, 4-6pm	2	ABA Consultant (trained by Casi)	$40 ($20/hour)
ABA Therapy: Sundays, 4-6pm	2	ABA Consultant (trained by Casi)	$40 ($20/hour)
ABA Therapy: Onsite at Childcare Center	1	ABA Consultant (trained by Casi)	$20 ($20/hour)
Speech Therapy: Local Early Intervention Agency	2 (2 sessions per week)	Speech Therapist	Subsidized by insurance and other sources
Occupational Therapy: Local Early Intervention Agency	2 (2 sessions per week)	Occupational Therapist	Subsidized by insurance and other sources
Chiropractor	1 (2 sessions per week)	Chiropractor	Paid lump sum for specific amount of sessions
Childcare (4 days per week)	~30		$1700/month
Total per week	**10.5 hours beyond Childcare and Chiropractor**		

Daniel: 3 Years – 4.75 Years:

After Daniel was three years old and started the special needs pre-school, Casi was in private practice. We discontinued childcare and started with an in-home nanny. Daniel's services included ABA therapy with additional home consultants, Pre-school, an Autism Extension Program with the school district, and Relationship-based Therapy.

Session Type	Hours	Therapist/ Consultant	Cost
ABA Therapy: Wednesdays, 6:00-7:30pm	1.5	Casi Olson	$120 ($80/hour)
ABA Therapy: Saturdays, 9-11am	2	Casi Olson	$160 ($80/hour)
ABA Therapy: Saturdays, 4-6pm	2	ABA Consultant (trained by Casi)	$40 ($20/hour)
ABA Therapy: Sundays, 4-6pm	2	ABA Consultant (trained by Casi)	$40 ($20/hour)
Relationship-Based Therapy (2 sessions/month)	.5	Occupational Therapist	$60 ($145/hour)
Pre-School Autism Extension Program (3 days/week)	6 (2 per day)		Free
Pre-school during school year (4 days/week)	10 (2.5 per day)		Free
Nanny Childcare	~25 hours	Nanny (trained by Casi as ABA Consultant)	$15/hour
Total per week	**24 hours beyond Childcare**		

Daniel: 4.75 – 5.5 years old

Changes: Casi moved to Minnesota, discontinued ABA Home Consultant, continued with Pre-school, discontinued the child-directed relationship based therapy. Our nanny was still working for us, applying ABA techniques. Casi occasionally provided a session.

Session Type	Hours	Therapist/ Consultant	Cost
ABA Therapy	2 hours per quarter	Casi Olson	$80/hour
School District Pre-school during school year (4 days per week)	10 (2.5 per day)	Pre-school Teacher	No cost to parents
School District Pre-School Social Group	2.5 (1 day per week)	Pre-school Teacher	No cost to parents
Nanny Childcare	~25 hours	Nanny	$15/hour
Total per week	**~12.5 hours per week beyond Childcare and quarterly ABA sessions**		

Daniel: 5.5 years old: Summer before Kindergarten
Changes: Jacob now a stay-at-home dad, with nanny helping as an ABA Consultant

Session Type	Hours	Therapist/ Consultant	Cost
Jacob (Father)	Unlimited	Jacob as a stay-at-home dad, implementing ABA techniques	Free
Nanny childcare	12 hours per week		
Horse-Riding Camp	4 day camp	Camp Team	$480 for the camp
Music Camp	4 day camp	Music Team	$250 for the camp
Soccer lessons	1 hour/week for 13 weeks	Coach	$160 for the term
Total	**~5 hours/ day of structured instruction while camps were active**		

- **Play Dates and ABA**

Carrie (Mother): I highly value the strategic play date. Casi helped us learn to utilize play dates as social therapy and ABA therapy for Daniel. I believe play dates have been very effective for helping him develop new communication skills. Below are some things I learned about how you can take advantage of play dates. In doing so, you are being an advocate for your child by helping them gain these new skills!

First of all, these play dates were strategic and were heavily facilitated by Casi to only enable functional and purposeful communication to emerge for Daniel. I loved these play dates and learned so much about how to be purposeful with Daniel during a play date...how to redirect him, how to prompt him to continue an interaction with the other child, and how to have patience through a meltdown but still enforce appropriate follow-through with Daniel so he could achieve success!

Secondly, I would invite another parent and child over for a play date, but explain that it was also going to be an ABA therapy session. There are many benefits from doing this. First, this makes it a safe place for you and your child. You have probably attended a play date where your child just didn't play well. Maybe you were stressed the whole time because your child wasn't behaving. By setting the stage with another mother/parent that this will be an intentional "practice" play date, the pressure is off of your child. Your child does not need to "perform" during the play date. He/she is going to work through some hard stuff. You've now created a safe place for your child.

You can also identify play date buddies from childcare, pre-school, or school. If your child can have extra time outside of school to build relationships with other kids from school, then when they go back to school they will see a familiar face and have a head start on building friendships. Excellent! Neighborhood friends are great, but try to find kids from your child's actual class. This was a tip I learned from another mother with a child diagnosed with autism.

Casi (Clinician): Play dates can be a helpful addition to a therapy program, especially as the child gets older and acquires more social skills. For children with autism, their comfort zone is with an adult because adults are more predictable, provide more consistent reinforcement for desirable social behavior, and quite frankly are probably what they are used to if they have been in therapy. Usually, kids with autism do not have the spontaneous desire to approach a peer and begin an interaction. This is where play dates come in! These opportunities give the child with autism the chance to learn that other children can be and are fun to play with. These play dates need to be facilitated by an adult to make sure the child with autism is rewarded for engaging in pro-social behavior; otherwise the child will not want to demonstrate it spontaneously.

Play dates can also be difficult for a parent to arrange. I equate it to dating for children, because it is all about finding the best fit. However, one of the most important components of a play date is to think about what is going to benefit your child the most. It is about finding a child who will complement your child and help them become exposed to situations and skills that are challenging for them. These play dates are not without challenge, but the results and progress that can be jumpstarted in your child are well worth the work.

Chapter Summary:

- In ABA efforts, you can set up a “home program” which can include other people being supervised by your ABA Home Program Supervisor. This can enable your money goes further in providing more hours of therapy for your child.
- If your child can master skills with different instructors, then it shows that your child is making great progress toward generalization.
- It is best if the parent can stay and observe the ABA therapy session.
- Tracking your hours of ABA Therapy and other therapies is helpful for communicating your overall services plan.
- Play dates can be a useful tool to help your child generalize their skills and work on social communication goals.

Chapter 8:
Fundamentals of Behavior

- **Determining the Behavior Sequence**

Casi (Clinician): At this point, I am sure the question "Okay, what do I use to change the behavior of a child with autism?" is being asked. The most reliable way of changing a behavior is through motivation (Rogers & Dawson, 2009). This involves preplanning and understanding the real reason why a behavior is there; meaning what is causing or triggering it and what is maintaining it or keeping it around. To figure this out, you need to identify what happens directly before the behavior you want to change, the "antecedent", determine exactly what the behavior is you want to change and what happens directly after the behavior occurs ("consequence") (Cooper et al, 2007). The events that occur directly after are the piece of the puzzle that tell you what is keeping the behavior alive. This information helps you determine a plan for how to eliminate the behavior. Does that child get out of eating their food if they begin to throw it, first? Does the child get to go to their room and be by themselves after they hit their sibling? This consequence category is directly related to our definition of discipline and whether or not it is truly appropriate for our child.

To start, let's review the antecedent, or what happens right before a child acts in a specific way. This period of time contains the triggers that make the behavior appear. In order to increase or decrease the chances the child will behave in a certain way, the trigger needs to be known.

Next, the actual behavior you want to stick around, or go away needs to be defined. It is important because all behavior can occur for different reasons, in different situations. The more information you have about what the child is doing, the better.

Lastly, the consequence needs to be identified. This is the period of time that occurs directly after a child demonstrates a behavior. In order for that behavior to keep going, a behavior-consequence relationship must be established. This means that a behavior must be demonstrated and then followed up with some kind of reward to increase the chance it will occur again. The word consequence can be misleading. All it means in this relationship is that it is the piece of the pie that controls if someone will act, or not act, in specific way. If a parent wants the behavior to keep happening then they will keep rewarding it. That includes toys, praise, stickers or anything the child is wanting. If the parent does not want the behavior to keep happening, they will take away whatever reward the child likes, or implement a punishment. These strategies can include a timeout, removal from a preferred activity or removing a desired toy from the child's possession. While these are all effective strategies, the child needs to be directly affected by the consequence; meaning that the child needs to be upset enough by the punishment to deter him or her from demonstrating the undesirable behavior again. The problem with this philosophy being utilized with children who have Autism Spectrum Disorders is that these consequences may not be important to them. One example is a timeout. This is technically referred to as a timeout from positive reinforcement, thus removing the child from a naturally motivating environment. If the core deficits of autism are highlighted such as challenges with social interaction and maintaining social engagement, along with wanting to be on their own, removing them from a situation and isolating them is not going to be a significant factor in changing their behavior. This is just one example of why punishment in its regular form is not a reliable way of changing the behavior of a child with autism. Instead, what could end up happening is the inadvertent reinforcement of a behavior that is not wanted because they are getting what they really want, alone time (Cooper et al, 2007).

The last important component to a behavior consequence relationship is reinforcement, or rewards. This can be anything the child wants! Rewards are one of the best ways to motivate the child to change their behavior. They are meant to be fluid and change frequently. I typically say that parents can provide their child with multiple options of rewards to see which one has the most 'power.' Then, if that reward begins to fade, move onto the next one! Rewards are meant to be fun and the 'golden ticket' to changing behavior.

- **Functions of Behavior**

A function of behavior is a technical way to explain why it is occurring. There are three main categories of reasons why we do what we do.

The first two are in relation to a person, situation, feeling/sensory stimulation or item. These are to escape or avoid, obtain or get an object or reaction and can occur within all settings. The third relates to a biological or medical need that is occurring within the person. An important thing to know about these categories is that one behavior can have all of the above functions, or many behaviors can have the same function. This makes it very tricky to tease apart why a child is doing what they are doing and makes it very important to figure out the why before a plan is put into place (Cooper et al, 2007).

Sometimes the reason behind behavior is not always logical or blindingly clear with children with autism. With Daniel, there was a point in time where Carrie and Jake would allow him to go to his room to "calm down" when he was upset or on the verge of a meltdown. Now, if this was a situation where the environment was over-stimulating for him, going to his room was a viable option. However, this was occurring during activities he did not want or when demands were placed on him. Instead of being a useful tool, it was rewarding his behavior because it gave him an "out" from the undesirable situation.

- **Extinction Bursts**

Casi (Clinician): The term Extinction Burst refers to the period of time after the reinforcement of a behavior is taken away and the child tries anything and everything to make that reinforcement come back. When a child is used to a specific reward to happen after they act in a certain way, it immediately does not seem right to the child. They then will "up the ante" to see what next level they need to bring their behavior to, to obtain the reward. This can go on for a very long time, with the behavior getting bigger in intensity, longer in duration and higher in frequency, like a "burst". This occurs until the child understands that the reward is not coming so therefore they should stop behaving in that way. By not providing them with the reward/reinforcement/maintaining element of the behavior, the behavior is eliminated. Now, there are certain behaviors, like some self-injurious and other harmful behaviors, that you do not want to let get bigger, longer or more frequent. I am not saying that parents should just let these behaviors happen, but instead of just taking away reinforcement, other components of skill teaching and safety need to be added to ensure there are no negative effects (Cooper et al, 2007).

During an extinction burst, it is important to follow through with not giving a reward. If the “missing” reward is provided during the time the child is increasing their behavior, the undesirable action is now stronger. This will send the message to the child that they just have to intensify and make their behavior bigger to get what they want. The next time they want that same reward, they will go right to that level of intense behavior. This makes it harder on the parent. Instead of “giving in,” parents can occupy themselves with something else, think happy thoughts, and do whatever is needed to do to follow through and not give in (Cooper et al, 2007)!

Chapter Summary:

- The key to changing a behavior is understanding what is rewarding it.
- Knowing what happens before and after a behavior is crucial to changing it
- When a behavior is not rewarded, it will get worse before it gets better

Chapter 9: Common Behavioral Challenges

Casi (Clinician): Within the diagnosis of autism, there is specific criteria that must be met. This criteria is directly related to how a child is behaving. To qualify for a diagnosis of autism under the fifth edition of the Diagnostic and Statistical Manual of Mental Disorders (DSM-5™), an individual needs to have "social communication and social interaction" deficits (Criteria A). The individual must also demonstrate at least 2 areas in which "repetitive, restrictive patterns of behavior, interests or activities" are observed (Criteria B). The symptoms must also be present in the early developmental timeframe. However, the symptoms can be behaviorally observed as the child gets older when they encounter new social demands. (American Psychiatric Association, 2013).

So, in other words, behaviors can be present in a child as soon as early childhood, but they can also be "triggered," so to say, by the presence of demands that are not able to be met therefore outpaces the person's ability to cope with those demands. What this all means is that every child with a diagnosis of autism will have different representations of the necessary criteria for a diagnosis to be given. Within each category of criteria qualification, there are different challenging behaviors that arise for each child. In this section, Carrie and I describe some of the possible behavioral concerns within each main criteria type from the DSM-5™ (American Psychiatric Association, 2013).

Carrie (Mother): You have likely already discovered that every child diagnosed with autism has their own unique combination of symptoms, behaviors, and challenges. While Daniel experienced a variety of autism-related behaviors to qualify him for a diagnosis, he did not exhibit all possible behaviors. In this chapter, Casi and I have attempted to describe some of the common behavioral and developmental challenges you might observe in a child on the spectrum. We also give examples of communication approaches that might manage or reduce these challenges.

Depending on your own mindset, adopting an ABA therapy approach may significantly alter an adult's communication style with a child diagnosed with autism. This was the case for me. I had to change the way I interacted with my son. I initially found many of the effective ABA approaches to be counter-intuitive, and against my natural instincts. I had to learn new communication skills, including the use of both words and gestures. My purpose for making these changes to my own communication style was to engage and encourage Daniel's efforts to master the typical early childhood development milestones.

Casi and I have not gone too deep into each challenge, but we want to give a brief overview for a few reasons:

1) So you know you are not alone in facing them
2) So that you can learn some of the behavior vocabulary
3) So that you might gain insights, regarding how ABA therapy concepts actually get applied to specific behavior challenges.

We provide the information in this chapter, like in the rest of the book, only to help guide you toward acquiring the right type of services for your child. Our strong recommendation, above all other recommendations, is to consult a qualified therapist for addressing your child's specific challenges.

Criteria A: <u>Social Communication and Social Interaction</u>

- Pretend Play Challenges
- Not Responding to Their Own Name
- Eye Contact Challenges
- Speech Challenges: Expressive Language
- Speech Challenges: Receptive Challenges
- Speech Challenges: Effects on Showing True Ability Level
- Conversation Challenges
- Lack of a Social Smile

(American Psychiatric Association, 2013; Rogers & Dawson, 2009).

- **Pretend Play Challenges**

Casi (Clinician): Whenever I ask a parent "what would you like to work on or what skill or behavior needs to change?" almost every single time they say, "I would LOVE it if she/he would play by themselves!" It is not a coincidence that this request comes up. Individuals with autism, especially children, have a difficult time entertaining themselves or engaging in self-directed play that stays appropriate or functional Cooper et al, 2007). This is due to the fact that they have inherent challenges in using their environment to dictate their behavior, meaning that it is difficult for them to approach a toy area on their own or pick out a toy or an activity and engage with it by themselves in a completely age appropriate and functional way. A child might pick up a toy and manipulate it in a way that provides them with self-stimulation, such as lining up objects, flicking a toy between their fingers, or waving an object in front of their eyes. These behaviors are not appropriate and functional to the toys and objects they are manipulating. Many times, parents will identify this method of play as silly and funny and cute and will not realize its significance in terms of developmental delay. These behaviors indicate an inability to interact with toys and materials in a functional and appropriate way that matches their chronological age (Rogers & Dawson, 2009).

Pretend play is a tricky one for kids with autism. To be able to pretend to be something else, an alternative perspective needs to be present; the grey area thinking of "yes, this yellow block can be used as hay for horses." This grey area thinking is not there: black and white, logical thinking is present, instead. A yellow block cannot be hay, because it is a yellow block. This way of thinking is not fun for kids because it is not logical, the expectations are not clear, and the steps to "pretend" are never the same; so predictability is out the window. Children with ASD need predictability, sameness, and clear expectations to make sense of their environment. Pretend play does not provide them with these qualities; therefore, it is difficult and uncomfortable for them and they simply are not interested. We need to make them interested and show them that it can be fun, especially with another person! It is all about expanding their interests and teaching them to do so in a way that makes sense to them. So, add in predictability, routine, and sequences; then fade them away once they begin to be interested.

Carrie (Mother): At the age of three, my child couldn't just "go play". I learned from Daniel's evaluations that Daniel's challenges prevented him from playing independently in an effective manner. It seemed as if it were almost more detrimental to allow him to engage in "play" on his own because it would just disintegrate into self-stimulatory or, or visually seeking behavior, or not be functionally appropriate. This aspect of parenting a child with autism is highly taxing. As the parent, you work to constantly engage the child, or direct and re-direct their play. You help them with learning and using words. You follow through with instruction and consequences when the meltdowns happen. In these early developmental years, Daniel needed Jake and me to guide him, coach him, redirect him, lead him, and teach him.

Because trains were a highly-preferred toy for Daniel, Casi helped us use his interest in trains to expand Daniel's ability to take part in pretend play. Other ways we worked to expand his pretend play with toys were to use a toy farm, a toy house, and other toys that could form the basis for a story.

Casi also gave us the idea to buy several different character costumes for Daniel so he could practice dressing up and pretend to be someone else. Essentially, we bought multiple Halloween costumes; but not because it was Halloween. This assumption of another identity was new territory for Daniel. He would enjoy it for a while, but if Jake and I kept up the act a little too long, we would know he was done when he said, "I'm just a Daniel". Pretend play was over, with that statement.

TIP for expanding play: At home, follow his play and expand on that by imitating what he is doing. Then, see if he will imitate you. However, when imitating his behavior in hopes he will imitate back, make sure to imitate only those actions appropriate to the activity in which he is engaged. Also, make the imitation exaggerated and exciting so he sees that you are interesting, too.

- **Not Responding to Their Own Name**

Casi (Clinician): Responding to their own name is one of the first skills that are targeted with someone who has an ASD diagnosis. Why is this so important? Well, logically we all know why. Responding to their name is how we know another person hears us, acknowledges us, or understands who they are. Without this skill, socializing and social communication with another person is almost impossible.

Individuals with autism struggle with this skill because its importance is not clear and apparent to those individuals who are not inherently motivated to interact with another person to get their needs met, gain another's perspective or to receive enjoyment through socially interacting. For most individuals who struggle with this skill, they are very consumed with their own thoughts and current actions that they are not aware that someone is trying to get their attention. Further, stopping what they are doing and attending to another person does not make sense to them. They like what they are doing, why stop? It is not seen as important, or in some cases, not a part of daily functioning because the reasoning behind it is not motivating to them. Most of us will not stop what we are doing to look at someone calling our name, if we don't really understand why it was important. Without this skill, social interaction can be extremely difficult.

How do you work on this skill then, if it is not motivating to the child to do so? Well, you make it motivating for them. You have an object that they want, you stand close to them and "get in their bubble," you say their name and when they look (with some prompting) you give them the preferred item you have. Now there are some other steps and description that can be included in this teaching sequence, but the general idea is to make responding to their own name interesting and exciting (Rogers & Dawson, 2009).

Carrie (Mother): One of the items that the clinical psychologist and Casi noted was that Daniel did not consistently respond to his name. It was difficult to truly get his attention. As his mother, I did not realize he was not responding to his name. He was still a baby to me, and I did not presume he should have immediate acknowledgement of his name or my requests of him. However, he should have been responding to his name.

As part of Daniel's initial ABA objectives, I found it enlightening that one of his goals was to get him to respond to his name. And how did we practice this? By measurements made in feet. This was probably my first true transition into ABA territory and the philosophies around it. We would challenge Daniel and measure his progress on responding to his name, first by the therapist (or parent or other initiator) being one foot away, then two feet, then three feet, then five feet, then ten feet. This was such a strange concept to me, that he didn't respond to his name, and that we could influence his response by practicing from certain distances. It was about expanding his level of awareness and the boundaries of the world in which he was living.

Was his world truly comprised of the items and activity within one foot of his body? Was he that locked in? Was autism taking that much of a hold of him that he was not aware of things beyond one foot? Yes, maybe so. How do we tear down those invisible walls that are locking him into his own world? How do we get him to see through them? We can see through them to him. Why can't he see through them to us? It was like a one-way window was in place around Daniel. Once I started understanding that, it helped me understand the ABA strategies more. I would have never conceived of that viewpoint myself.

In addition, the idea that we should not even try to talk to Daniel from another room was very enlightening to me. This new requirement was a significant behavior change for our family. We had to dispel any expectation that he might respond to us. I think it's very common that you might call out to your husband or child from the kitchen while they are in a bedroom down the hall, or from the kitchen while they are even in the next room. You might expect and that they will hear you and potentially respond. However, I learned that Daniel was not responding to this type of remote information. With one of his early ABA goals to get a response from Daniel at a distance of one foot from him, Jake and I came to understand that there was no way that we could try to give him instruction (not even using his name) from a completely different room. Even in the car, with me driving in the front seat and Daniel in his car seat behind me, I had to give up expecting a response, until Daniel gained some new skills.

I laugh to myself now when Daniel yells down the hall for me to get him something or makes some other request. Or, I can call to him and he quickly responds. We have come a very long way, but we literally started at one foot.

TIP: When you say your child's name, always follow through with engaging them! Never let that opportunity pass; otherwise, the idea that it is not an important part of communicating will be rewarded (Cooper et al, 2007).

TIP: Don't try to get your child's attention by calling to them from another room where the TV is on and other people are also talking. You should try to have the child respond to you in the same room, even from just 1 or a few feet away, with no other distractions interfering with your communication to them. Start close to them and build the distance. Your child truly may not "hear" you trying to get their attention. They are likely not purposefully ignoring you. When the child does turn to you and make eye contact, give them a positive "reward," like a toy to play with or a little treat (Daniel loved chocolate chips).

- **Eye Contact Challenges**

Casi (Clinician): As a professional, I see a lack of eye contact as a sign both that it is uncomfortable for the child and that they are unaware that it is a social expectation to make eye contact while interacting. A possible solution: require them to make eye contact during socially appropriate times when the common expectation is to make eye contact. This can be to indicate interest in an object, while giving and taking, or while communicating wants and needs.

I have seen children and adolescents make fleeting eye contact when they know it is expected. It is up to the treatment team to decide when fleeting eye contact is acceptable and when it is not. Every situation is different and can be influenced by culture as well. The influence of culture is something to take into consideration when teaching a skill like eye contact. The social appropriateness should always be determined when goal writing any social interaction or communication skill (Cooper et al, 2007).

Tip: Keep waiting for their eye contact before giving them what they want, and always play face-to-face.
TIP: While reading books and singing songs, wait for their eye contact before continuing.
TIP: Encourage them to ask for things rather than getting them by pointing alone.
TIP: Always require a little more once your they demonstrate consistency with one mode of communicating.

- **Speech Challenges: Expressive Language**

Casi (Clinician): Almost every parent talks about either a speech delay or lack of speech as a point of worry for them. When this happens, the focus is "what happened?" "We need to help him talk, interpret his behaviors, know what he wants." From my perspective, the best thing to do is think "how can we help him/her learn that communicating is essential to everyday life." The first thing I do is recommend that the parents seek assistance from a Speech and Language Pathologist. Then, the team can write goals around the specific speech challenges your child has.

Expressive language communication challenges are those that involve the actual production of speech and how a thought is conveyed. Sometimes there is a delay or speech organization deficit. On other times, there are children who do not have words or produce minimal words. Regardless of what specific type of speech challenge my clients have I emphasize the communicative opportunities in each social interaction (the amount of times we allow or require them to communicate to get their needs met) and how to increase these chances throughout a child's everyday life. Instead of anticipating what you think they want, make them communicate it through eye contact, sounds, gestures, or words. When they communicate in the desired way, give them more of what they were asking for. This is to show them that communicating using multiple kinds of strategies such as eye contact, gestures and words, are the way to get what they want, more of it, and faster. In other words, teach them to communicate using more appropriate methods, as indicated above, instead of hitting, crying, whining, throwing, or remaining silent (Cooper et al, 2007).

I like to focus on the communicative opportunities right away in my work with a child. This means that I do a lot of parent coaching around not anticipating what their child wants, but instead "playing dumb," to flush out exactly what their child is desiring. Then, I require the child to communicate for everything they want and need throughout their day. This includes their interactions with their parents, siblings, aunts, uncles, everyone. When I say communicate, I mean utilizing whatever language skill level they are working on. This could be eye contact to start, or a gesture, or a sign or 3 word phrases. It all depends on each individual child. An important component to addressing any speech challenge is having a speech therapist on the team. This ensures that speech deficits of any nature are addressed appropriately and progress is maximized (Rogers & Dawson, 2009).

- **Speech Challenges: Receptive Language**

Casi (Clinician): The other side of speech is processing or understanding what is being communicated to a person, or what they take in (receptive language). Some children I work with can receptively understand much more than their expressive language indicates. An example is when a child can follow a one-step command such as "sit down," but cannot say the words "sit down." Also, there will be times when processing the language or type of communication will be slow. This is a receptive language difficulty, because it is how fast the person takes in information used in communication. Early on in my career, I worked with a boy who needed an extra couple of seconds to process what we were asking of him before he responded. In the beginning though, he would become frustrated when we prompted him immediately after a request because he did not do what we asked of him. His frustration was a sign that we needed to look deeper into how he was processing his demands. Just keep in mind though that any speech-related difficulty should be treated with the guidance of a speech therapist, even if goals are written within an ABA home therapy setting.

- **Speech Challenges: Effects on Showing True Ability Level**

Casi (Clinician): Where expressive and receptive language meets is where another area of difficulty is present. This is true when we are determining a child's cognitive ability. If a child understands what is being said to them and knows they need to answer a specific question, then their true ability level is shown. If all or parts of that sequence is not present, then it is difficult to get a good grasp on what the child knows and doesn't know. A lot of the time, a child's true cognitive ability is not known because these test cognition utilizing standardized tests, which utilize many aspects of expressive and receptive language. There are many children who do score well on those tests - awesome! What do we do for those children who do not; or who are unable to show those cognitive skills because of their specific language challenges? We take a step back and determine what their barriers are to demonstrate their true ability. Establishing a clear path from point A to B can be useful when teaching skills to children with autism (Cooper et al, 2007). When cognitive challenges arise, it sometimes indicates that the child really does not understand what is being asked of them or it indicates that they do not have the language ability to communicate their knowledge with you. Many of us have had this thought, "If only I understood what was being asked of me, I could be successful." The same is true here.

Carrie (Mother): Around 17 or 18 months old, Daniel stopped gaining words. I think that we didn't really realize he was not gaining words because he did have some words he was using. However, looking back, his progress slowed down.

Near the time of Daniel's diagnosis (28 months), he had been in speech therapy for about 5-6 weeks. One of the things the speech therapist suggested was keeping a word list of the words Daniel voluntarily spoke in an unprompted manner. Oh, we were so hungry to hear new words from Daniel as we created the list. We were listening and counting every word we heard Daniel say. Below is the list of words we captured that Daniel would say when he was 28 months old. The word list is about 70 words total. This is, truly, an exhaustive list of words he freely spoke near the time he began speech therapy.

Thomas	Apple	All Aboard	Dadda
Engine	Moon	McQueen	Nigh Nigh
Track	Star	Mack	Ashes
More	Diamond	James	Book
All Done	Up	Ba Ba	Road
All Gone	Down	Nana	Whale
Juice	Snack	Papa	Eye
Milk	Choo Choo	Momma	Mouth
Five	Nine	Two	Big
Go	Stop	Gosh	Look
Oh no	Oh man	Wheel	Boo
Joe	Daniel	Show	Elmo
Where	Bump	Bye bye	No bite
Hot	Bubble	Teeth	Button
Nose	Feet	Noise	Scoop
Cheers	Bridge	Stuck	Beach
Fish	Happy	Open	Bike
Water	Wet	Button	Trash
Snowman	Buzz	Sleep “seep”	Gate

Carrie (Mother): From her review of these words, what the speech therapist observed about this list is that it is mostly nouns, or labels. Our speech therapist pointed out that there were very few verbs or “connector” words. The speech therapist helped us understand that we had to help Daniel learn some of the connector words before he could demonstrate functional language. This observation was very eye-opening to me, and not something I noticed on my own. Once it was pointed out to me, it was very apparent and made a lot of sense.

We then learned the technique of “one-upping” in the use of speech. When Daniel was only using one-word phrases, we were only allowed to use two words (Brown, 1973). So if he could say "car", we would say "Car roll" and play with a car while rolling it. When he learned to say "car roll" or "top on" or "top off", we could then say "car roll fast" or "car roll slow" or "take top off" or "put top on". You "one-up" the child from the level of speech they can currently complete. You don't jump ahead and just continue speaking to them in full sentences. The child cannot process all of that information yet.

This one-upping technique actually took me a lot of practice and it was difficult to slow myself down enough to just one-up. It was more natural for me to speak to Daniel in full sentences. I had to break that habit and learn a new way to communicate with Daniel, as he had delays in both expressive and receptive language. You can search online for examples of using two-word utterances and two-word combinations that can help you communicate with your child in a way that may be more effective than in full sentences (Brown, 1973). Your child can hear you, but they may need to hear at a slower pace in order to comprehend. I had to learn this about Daniel.

TIP: It is important to consider how many words you are expecting your child to understand when you are talking to them. Therefore, reduce the amount of words to 1-2 words more than what they are producing, keeping the phrases short and to the point: no "fluffy" talk (Rogers & Dawson, 2009).
TIP: Provide lots of narration when interacting with your child (i.e., "oh, up up up and down down down" while flying a plane in the air), make sound effects while playing, and see if the child will imitate the sounds (Rogers & Dawson, 2009).
TIP: Make lots of comments instead of asking lots of questions: "It's a ____, I see a _____." Hold back words in favorite routines and require the child to fill them in; be excited when they do (Rogers & Dawson, 2009)!
TIP: If language production is an issue, write all words your child produces spontaneously or in imitation, because service providers will want to know (Rogers & Dawson, 2009)!

TIP: When singing a song, pause before saying the last word of a phrase. See if your child will fill in the blank to keep the song going. This may help your child demonstrate that he/she knows the song but cannot produce all the words at the speed the song requires (Rogers & Dawson, 2009).

Twinkle, Twinkle Little _________ <wait for your child>

How I Wonder What You _____________ <wait for your child>

Up Above the World So ______________ <wait for your child>

Like a Diamond in the ________________ <wait for your child>

- **Conversation Challenges**

Casi (Clinician): Social skills (or the lack thereof) is a huge focus of any therapeutic treatment. In kids with autism, social skills deficits lie in both the way they express and receive social input. It is difficult for them to understand the hidden social skills of a setting or environment, and therefore the way that they make sense of it all is by memorizing certain people or pieces of that environment that they can recall when they enter into a new setting. The end goal of each child's skill development is for them to read the hidden social cues and skills in any social situation, and be able to adjust their behavior accordingly. To get to that point, one must break down basic social behavior in a systematic, predictable way that each child can then take with them as they go throughout their day. Some examples of some basic social skills that individuals with autism are taught include personal space, body orientation by contact, on topic versus off topic, loudness of voice, and conversations (Cooper et al, 2007; Rogers & Dawson, 2009).

It is not uncommon that a parent believes their child already has adequate social skills in some of these areas, because they know their child and they can read their child. The only way to truly tell if the child is changing their social behavior is if they are able to demonstrate these skills in all environments with all different types of people (see Chapter 4, Fundamentals of ABA, for more information about generalization). When a child is learning how to interact with others, it takes some adjustment time. This skill set does not come naturally to many individuals, and at times seems robotic. This robotic presentation indicates that to learn these skills, very structured black and white social scripts need to be created in each child (Cooper et al, 2007).

For example, if we are teaching a child how to have a natural productive conversation, including many "back and forths" with someone else, a special written script needs to be given to the child to outline the expectations that the child has for the social interaction. "Back and forths" in a conversation indicate the component of a conversation in which one person asks a question, and the other person answers. For example "Hi, How are you? How was your weekend? My weekend was great. Have a nice day." A sample script like this is needed until the child can approach a familiar person and initiate this type of conversation spontaneously.

Recently I arranged a social 'hangout' between two of my male clients who are working on appropriate conversation and social skills in their sessions with me. Right before they met each other, I had each of them write out how they will start a conversation and what questions they will ask the other boy. I was present to facilitate the interaction, but required them to reference their 'scripts' throughout the conversation when they looked stuck, or did not know what to say next. After a few conversations like this, they began to initiate and maintain their own conversations spontaneously, without the scripts in hand.

These social skills are taught either one-on-one or in a group social setting, like my example above. Social skills can be taught one on one with an adult first; then transferred into a small group setting to promote generalization with peers. The only way to truly know if a child can utilize the skills taught in a natural setting is to facilitate this type of interaction and teach in the moment. Not every area of social communication needs a script for each child. Every child with autism requires different systems to teach the skills they need.

Carrie (Mother): If I were out running errands with Daniel, when he would see another child, he would not engage them in a typical way. I remember being in a large toy store, and Daniel was in the seat in the cart. If we passed by another child, he would essentially roar at them. This became a common behavior. Of course, most kids did not respond back to Daniel with appropriate conversation. They would generally not respond at all. He wasn't trying to scare these kids. He was trying to get their attention. It became apparent to me that he was trying to engage them, but he just didn't know the words to say. He didn't know how to get them to interact, but he craved the interaction. My natural reaction as an untrained parent is to laugh off his "roar" and say something like, "Daniel, don't yell at him." It was a little embarrassing. I would just keep pushing the cart toward another aisle. However, thanks to ABA and Casi's guidance, we were able to practice role play and gave Daniel new phrases he can use to start up a conversation with another child.

I still remember the first conversation I observed in public between Daniel and another person without having to step in. Daniel was about almost 4 years old, and I was a solid seven months pregnant with Caleb. We were at a local shopping center getting some fabric for Caleb's nursery. Before we went in the store, Daniel wanted to play on these big rocks that are part of the landscaping. As we were playing near the rocks, Daniel pointed out that bees were in the plants. He and I were just hanging out. Then a father and his three kids (elementary age, older than Daniel) came up to wait for the shuttle to the zoo. They sat down on a bench near where Daniel was watching the bees. Daniel walked over to them! The father started talking to Daniel, asking him some questions. Seeing my belly, this man asked him about him becoming a big brother. Daniel started answering his questions. Daniel told him he was going to have a little brother. Daniel started telling this man about the bees, as well. Daniel even said some things that made the older siblings giggle a little. The father was very sweet, but was not overly accommodating to Daniel in the conversation. The father didn't have to repeat himself. Daniel helped keep the conversation going.

During this whole time, I did not step in to help Daniel navigate this conversation. I did not need to. I was nervous he would stumble, but he didn't. I was about 10-15 feet from where they were talking, and I could hear them, but I was not part of the conversation. I just smiled and listened to their discussion. I felt like I had a big secret I wasn't sharing. I felt so proud of Daniel, and felt so "normal."

I didn't have to make excuses for him. I didn't have to answer for him. This family just thought they were talking to a typical 3-(almost 4)-year-old. I just watched, as a little experiment; but I wanted to shout to this family, "You don't know how hard we've worked for you to just have a conversation about bees, and the big rock, and Daniel about to have a new baby brother!! You'll never know. And I kind of love that! But this is such a major moment for Daniel! He just answered multiple questions without prompting! He volunteered information about the bees without prompting! Your kids thought he was funny! This is such a milestone for us."

- **Lack of a Social Smile**

Casi (Clinician): The social smile stands out to me as a professional. It's a behavior I work very hard to develop and obtain in a child. Once achieved, it can spark hope in parents that they might connect with their child in a meaningful way.

A social smile is a skill that children use to bring another person into their play, actions, and thoughts. This component of social communication keeps a play partner interested in the child's activity because it gives the play partner a social reward (Rogers & Dawson, 2009).

Along with Carrie and Jake, many parents have expressed confusion around this topic of a social smile. The reason is because every parent has a connection with their child. While each connection looks different from one parent/family to another, it is still there. However, this connection is not transferred into every other social interaction with individuals outside of their immediate family. What individuals with autism struggle with is returning a smile in response to a coy or teasing look, a playful interaction, or a shared enjoyment with another person when referencing an activity. It's that smile a child gives when saying,

"Look mom, I built this tower!" The social smile is a different smile than the smile one gives when their needs are simply being met.

Carrie (Mother): By the time Daniel was 5½ years old, Daniel developed a social smile that showed up more easily. How did he develop this along the way? I believe his level of environmental awareness increased because of the therapies Daniel received and the dietary changes. His sense of humor began to develop. Once he started making progress in the area of "shared enjoyment", his social smile started making an appearance.

TIP: Create social opportunities for your child, regardless of age or skill level (Rogers & Dawson, 2009).

TIP: Talk to his schoolteachers or childcare teachers to learn if there are kids who already like to play with your child. Invite them over and encourage your child to do one social thing that is out of his comfort zone (Rogers & Dawson, 2009). For example, you can request your child initiate a conversation about what they did that day, or merely have him share a few predetermined toys and work on his social flexibility with another child, playing with their toys .

TIP: To encourage the social smile, begin with preferred toys and be silly and fun with them! Make it look fun to play the way you are playing and draw the child's attention to your actions through the preferred toy. When a social smile is present, provide over-the-top social praise and positive interactions that your child likes such as tickles, squishes, wrestling, or swinging upside down (Rogers & Dawson, 2009).

Criteria B: Restricted, Repetitive Patterns of Behavior, Interests, or Activities

- Preferred Toys (strong preferences)
- Self-stimulatory Behavior ("stimming")
- Rigidity and Inflexibility to Change Challenges
- The Need for Perfection
- Anxiety, OCD, and Depression Challenges
- Sensory Integration Challenges
- Aggression (Impulse Control) Challenges
- Self-Injurious Behavior (SIB)

(American Psychiatric Association, 2013; Rogers & Dawson, 2009).

- **Echolalia**

Casi (Clinician): Echolalia is one of the most common forms of speech in children with autism. It is the act of repeating or "parroting" what another person is saying. It is not typically used in a functional manner, but as an immediate echo. Also, the child does not direct it at a person, like in a conversation, and the child utilizes the same tone, intensity and volume as the person who originally said the word/phrase. The most important thing to remember is that echolalia is not considered functional speech, meaning that that speech therapy can assist a child in developing a more functional way to communicate (DSM-5™ Diagnostic Criteria, 2017).

Carrie (Mother): Daniel experienced echolalia to a small degree, but it was there, and still is a bit even now. When he was newly diagnosed, it became apparent to us that he would often repeat the last word of the question you asked him. For example: to the question, "Is this a train?" He would answer "Train". Or, to the comment, "Look, it's James!" Daniel would say "James". So, it could seem as though he is interacting, but really he is just repeating the last word or phrase stated. This is another enlightening thing to observe in your child, once you can identify it. And for me, it was another unwelcome awakening to some of the challenges my son was facing.

More recently, he will still sometimes repeat sentences or words others are saying when he may not know what to say himself. For example, when I ask him to talk on the phone to his grandmother, he may just repeat the questions she asks him, rather than appropriately answering the questions to continue the conversation. Casi has helped me understand that this still echolalia, but it is showing up a little differently than it did before when he was younger.

Rather than me getting upset with Daniel for "joking around" too much and "being rude" to the person on the phone, I need to realize that he just needs more coaching about how to communicate appropriately in a phone conversation.

TIP: If your child is repeating the last thing you say and you are not sure what their real answer is, try switching up the choices. For example, start with "Do you want the red or green?" first, then switch it to "Do you want the green or red?", or "Do you want the red or green train?" This technique varies the options at the end of the question so that you can assess if your child is truly answering it, or simply repeating the last word or phrase.

- **Preferred Toys (Strong Preferences)**

Casi (Clinician): One of the things every parent tells me is that their child "loves" one specific toy. Whether it is trains, cars, letters, or things that turn, these objects are things that the child wants with them all the time, regardless of its appropriateness to the activity. While all children go through phases of loving Lightening McQueen or Thomas the Train, these are just phases, and typically pass within months. For children and individuals with ASD, these interests typically do not pass within months. They develop into attachment items and fixations and the focused interest does not transfer to other toys. These "preferred toys," are not allowed to be played with by any other child or people. They trigger meltdowns and challenging behaviors because the child is unable or unwilling to part with them. And the usual negotiation and reasoning skills parents utilize during these situations do not work. This is where the toy is more than just a "current favorite."

When this occurs, it would be considered a restrictive area of interest because the child will not interact appropriately with any other object or toy and requires that they have a specific item instead. To address this, behavior strategies would be put in place to teach both coping skills around not having that specific object and interest in other objects and toys (Cooper et al, 2007; DSM-5™ Diagnostic Criteria, 2017).

Carrie (Mother): By 12 months, we knew Daniel loved anything that was round and spun, or any toy with buttons. I remember requesting toys like this for his first birthday. By 18 months, Daniel was very into Thomas trains: So much so that we bought a Thomas toddler bed for him at 18 months when he started climbing out of his crib.

Daniel could play with trains 24/7.

In our therapy sessions, we identified what was "most preferred" by Daniel. Then, we purposefully restricted access to most preferred items to allow and encourage other interests to evolve. For example: while trains were by far Daniel's favorite toys, we began to limit both his time spent with them and his access to them. We put all of the trains and tracks in a couple of bins that we placed high on a bookshelf or in a cabinet where he could not see them or reach them. We would bring them out only at certain times and for limited duration.

We were working to "expand" his play. One of the things we were trying to do as part of expanding his play was work to develop new interests in other types of toys beyond trains. When he wasn't playing with trains, we would encourage him to play with less-preferred toys such as race cars or a farm toy or a kitchen toy. We tried to introduce toys around which we could build a story.

TIP: when there is a toy or object that your child is attached to, you can practice restricting access to that toy. It is not about taking it away forever, it is about allowing it when the time is appropriate and helping your child calm down when they cannot have it. This can be done through redirection, teaching of coping and calm down strategies (such as deep breathing, counting, etc.), and not giving in once you have set the boundaries and expectations of when they can and cannot have their "favorite toy" (Garland, 2014).

TIP: Before moving on to play with a preferred toy, you can direct your child to continue play with a non-preferred toy "one more time", or take "one more turn" in a game, before moving on to the preferred activity. This exercise helps expand a child's flexibility and teaches him how to follow an agenda.

- **Self-Stimulatory Behavior ("Stimming")**

Casi (Clinician): Self-stimulatory behavior makes a regular appearance in individuals with autism. Most of the time, this behavior is shown in place of functional or appropriate ways of interacting with toys or other materials. It may seem odd or illogical; however, it satisfies a specific sensory need within that person. Most of the time we cannot see how that specific self-stimulatory behavior how someone feels is considered a private event or sensations only that person has. No one else knows exactly how that specific behavior feels for that specific person (Cooper et al, 2007).

However, we can teach an individual how to control the impulse and reserve the self-stimulatory behavior for a more appropriate time. This is important because the need for self-stimulatory behavior will always be there due to the feeling it is giving that person. It will not just go away if that specific behavior is "stopped." The sensory stimulation component to the behavior will always need to be met in some way.

Carrie (Mother): From the initial onsite childcare evaluation of Daniel by our local early intervention agency, I remember that the evaluator noticed Daniel engaging in "visually seeking" activities. This was the first time I'd heard the term "visually seeking". That would explain the types of activities he enjoyed like spinning wheels on a truck rather than rolling the truck through the mud or on a road. It was common behavior for Daniel to lie down to play with his toys, even when I knew he wasn't tired. He would just lie there calmly and look at a truck or train very closely. He might turn the wheel with his finger or roll the object back and forth, but not with meaningful motion. Or he might be at a table rolling a train, but would put his forehead down on the train...so he wasn't actually looking at the train, but was more resting his forehead on it. It turns out that this behavior means he was watching how the toys moved rather than actually playing with the toys in play, or pretend, scenarios. He would focus on specific parts of toys, not the whole toy. He would move the toy in a way that stimulated his visual field or other senses, but this interaction is not considered typical play for a toddler.

Another thing that Daniel did, which I notice more after his diagnosis, was that he would flap his right hand occasionally. He would do this when he was happy and excited, or also when he was very frustrated. But for Daniel, it was mostly when he was happy. This was a behavior I did not have eyes for until after his diagnosis. When he was excited and happy, he would begin flapping his right hand. Usually, it was when he was listening to music or watching something that was very animated. He would be having a good time.

When I saw Daniel flapping his hands, I definitely had mixed emotions. It was a reminder to me that the diagnosis was real; something I could not deny. On the other hand, it was a sign to me that he was in a good mood; that he was having a good time. It made me happy for him, to know he was enjoying himself.

TIP: When self-stim behavior begins, redirect without adding a negative consequence. Then develop a plan to help increase a level of control for that individual, if it's appropriate to the situation. This means that a child could be given self-stim "breaks" where they can engage in the behavior, and then at the end of the break, they need to stop or disengage from it (Cooper et al, 2007).

- **Sensory Integration Challenges**

Casi (Clinician): Sensory integration challenges are common in children with autism. If there are challenges, either over- or under-sensitivity occurs among some or all of the five senses. It has to do with how individuals process their environment and the input they receive from it. A few examples on the sensitivity spectrum include a high pain tolerance or an extreme cold temperature threshold. An individual's ability to have awareness of their body is a factor in how sensory input affects behavior (Cooper et al, 2007).

Carrie (Mother): When Daniel was younger, loud noises and bright lights would cause him to get very upset.

Sound sensitivity: Here are several examples:

- Household Appliance Noises: When I ran the vacuum or the blender, Daniel would break down and start crying. I learned to warn Daniel when I was going to start the vacuum, and he would either go to his room or I would set him up on the couch with pillows so he could cover his ears. It was the same for the blender. I would have to warn him that I was going to start it, and it was torture for him to endure the sound.
- Retail Store Noises: Another example I experienced with Daniel's sound sensitivity was going into a party store, where they were blowing up balloons using a helium machine as we were standing in line to check out. The sound of the helium filling the balloon caused Daniel to cry and become very anxious. Each time this

happened, it surprised me. Things you might never think of as "noise pollution" would bring my child to the brink of hysteria.

- Public Restroom Noises: If your child is sensitive to loud noises, you may learn to hate automated features in public restrooms. For example, on automated toilets, you cannot control the flush. Daniel would be very sensitive to the sound of a flushing toilet as well as the sound of the automated hand dryer. As a mother, you learn to love all the manual restroom features. Daniel did not like the sounds but did not refuse to use public restrooms. I would just have to talk him through it and figure out alternatives to the hand dryer or other noisy things. I would have to warn him about the flushing noise. I remember Casi being very happy to hear that he would go into the public restrooms even though he didn't like it. Progress!

Light Sensitivity: Here are a couple examples:

- Lights in the House: In the mornings, it would take him a good 15 minutes to adjust to the light after waking up in the morning. We happened to have dimmers in his bedroom and in our bedroom, so we would start the lights on the lowest settings. He would get in our bed and get under the covers, saying, "Too bright, too bright". There would be barely any lights on.
- Sunlight in the Car: As a baby in his car seat, he would cry and protest when the sun would shine in on him through the window. He did not like the sun, and his cries truly seemed as though he was in pain when the sun would hit him. This sensitivity to the light and the sun continued as he aged. When he was about 14-18 months old, he would express that his eyes were very sensitive to light. When he was old enough, I would hand him a towel in the car so that he could cover his face and head when the sun would shine on him in the car. He would self-regulate his usage of the towel. This was simply how we did things.

TIP: For sensory integration challenges, it is all about systematically getting the child used to the offending input that sends them into overload. Take it minute by minute: 1 minute with the noise on (example: a vacuum), 10 minutes with it off. Provide visuals to help them understand when the noise will start, how long it will take, and when it will end (Cooper et al, 2007).

- **Rigidity and Inflexibility to Change Challenges**

Casi (Clinician): One huge differentiation that needs to be addressed when a challenging behavior arises is whether or not the behavior is attributable to anxiety or sensory related concerns, or if it's purely behavioral. In this section, we will discuss the rigidity and inflexibility that some children with autism demonstrate. Even though we have separated these sections out, the concepts are intertwined. Sometimes a behavior starts out as rigidity, but then has anxiety and sensory related components as you progress through it. Please keep that in mind when trying to figure out where your child's behavior 'fits.'

When looking at your child's behavior, I am sure there are things they do that bug you or are a nuisance, such as eating with their mouths open, tapping their hands on the table or swinging their legs around when sitting in a chair. These behaviors are not necessarily the ones you absolutely need to change to better their quality of life. Most of the time rigid behaviors start out seeming very benign. The big picture message involves determining which behaviors pose a problem to your child's ability to appropriately and effectively interact with other people and their environment. Some examples of these types of behaviors include the following:

- The child insisting that they sit on one side of car and becoming upset if requested to sit on the other side

- The child needing to have breakfast before getting clothes on every morning and becomes upset if things are reversed

- The child eating only a specific kind of chicken nugget, and refusing other foods

These types of behaviors may seem harmless, but what makes them concerning is when they stop the child from functioning if a particular situation does not occur a specific way.

Once you determine the behaviors that pose a problem, the therapist can create a plan of action! The therapist will analyze the behavior working to answer questions like:

- What is the reason they are doing what they are doing?

- How do we help them communicate their needs better?

Every behavior has a reason behind it, such as attention, avoidance, or sensory input. Identification of the reason enables the therapist (with your input) to determine how to help your child. See Chapter 8, Fundamentals of Behavior, for more information.

Carrie (Mother): Casi was so supportive in helping us get Daniel past his shoe rigidity. Putting on the same pair of shoes each day is an easy habit to fall into with a toddler. When Daniel was between 12-24 months, we would change his shoes. I guess his feet were growing fast, so we got new ones and would put different pairs on him. He didn't care what shoes he wore. However, we fell into a routine when Daniel was a little over 2 years old, of just putting on the same shoes each day. They were a pair of cute shoes that were slip on, with elastic laces. When the laces on one of the shoes broke, we got him a new pair of shoes that was a different brand.

Daniel would have nothing to do with the new shoes. He would throw a tantrum and wanted to take off the new shoes. It was as if they were hurting him. He would only wear the old pair of the preferred pair of shoes. So, what did we do? We went out and found another size 7 of the same original shoes. I also had the laces repaired on the first pair. We then bought the next size up of those same blue/black/white shoes. And then we pre-bought the next size after that. And the next size after that. So, we ended up with two pairs of size 7's, three pairs of size 8's, one pair of size 9's, and one pair of size 10's, in those shoes.

Getting Daniel to tolerate and accept multiple different styles of shoes was one of the major early accomplishments in our ABA therapy. We let Casi know about this shoe challenge early in our ABA sessions. She made one of our goals in therapy to be getting Daniel able to wear other pairs of shoes. Casi asked us to get a different pair of shoes that we would work toward having him wear successfully. We picked a pair of shoes to work on, with him. We chose shoes that were totally different. They were all white and lace up, not the slip-on type.

Daniel would cry and fight against the less preferred shoes, when we would attempt to put them on him. Casi helped us understand that his distress was not about how the shoes felt on him; it was him having the knowledge that he was wearing shoes that were different from his most preferred ones.

Casi let us know that this was an anxiety-related behavioral issue, not a sensory issue. She taught us how to work up his tolerance to less preferred shoes. We would put the shoes on and hold up our hand and count our fingers down for 5 seconds. Then, we'd take the shoes off. Each day, we had him wear the shoes for five seconds. The goal was to have him tolerate the shoes, but he knew that the shoe-wearing would come to an end. This method provides the child with an end in sight, and it gives him a visual of the actual time that it will take until the shoes come off. As he got more comfortable with 5 seconds, we then would move the time up to ten seconds, then 15, then 20. What's interesting is that as we moved the time up and Daniel would tolerate it, once we got to about 30-45 seconds, Daniel would temporarily forget about the shoes. Once we almost got out the door to get in the car before he realized he was still wearing the less preferred shoes. We applied this method for several weeks, working up to 2 minutes and beyond…and then one day we were able to show up to an ABA session with Casi and silently point out to her which shoes he was wearing. He had forgotten that the "wrong" shoes were on his feet. This was a major accomplishment for him, and for us! This was a main method of how we worked with Daniel to increase his flexibility with his environment and decrease his need for rigidity.

After more weeks of the desensitization process on the offensive shoes, a major turning point happened when I took Daniel into the shoe store to see if he would pick a new pair of shoes for himself. The illustration below is of pair similar to those he decided on. They were darker coloring and a familiar cartoon character on them, along with a strap closure. Daniel even wanted to wear them out of the store! That is what I call progress!

An example of another success with Daniel's increased flexibility came when he was just over four years old. At that time he had developed a preference for no collars and no buttons on his shirts, for daytime clothes. However, for some reason, he was not opposed to wearing pajamas that had a collar and buttoned-up front. I was getting clothes out for church and decided to “test” Daniel’s rigidity by offering him the choice of two collared shirts to pick from. I described them, and I said casually that one of them was a lot like a “pajama top” (which he would wear). He picked that one and wore it to church! This was a new accomplishment!

- **Challenges Dealing with Transitions**

Casi (Clinician): Transitions with kids are tough, in general. However, with children with autism, there is an extra level of difficulty. Part of the transition process involves change from one routine/situation/location into a new one. This would require the individual to survey this new "something" to see what their expected behavior is going to be. It requires the ability to change behavior based on the social surroundings around the individual. One of the deficits of autism is this exact ability. It induces anxiety and therefore evokes behaviors to cope with this anxiety. So, what do you do about this? Provide structure to help your child know what is going to happen. And, if the unexpected occurs, help establish coping mechanisms (Cooper et al, 2007).

In my sessions with children struggling with transitions, I typically add a visual schedule to the session structure to help alleviate some of the transitional difficulties. However, I change up the schedule to help the child cope with a change in the routine. It is all about helping the child be more adaptable in 'real life' circumstances, which then helps them and their parents when daily activities change spur of the moment.

Carrie (Mother): A major challenge Daniel faced before beginning ABA therapy was enduring transitions from one activity to another. He would get fixated on a preferred activity, and it was very difficult for Jake and me to redirect him. Playing with trains was the central preferred activity for Daniel at the time of his diagnosis. If he spotted a train table in a store or in a doctor's office, watch out. He would want nothing else, and he was not able to be consoled easily. Through the ABA therapy work with Daniel, we had to learn what "redirect" meant, and we learned skills for re-directing Daniel. The ABA therapy also focused on helping Daniel gain new emotion self-regulation skills so that he could become easier to console. He needed to develop coping mechanisms for getting through these unwanted transitions (beyond biting).

An example of when I was unable to console Daniel through a transition was on a trip to the grocery store. I took Daniel with me to the store. There were real, but abandoned, train tracks near the store. He saw these out of the car window when we drove into the parking lot. I thought, "I'll let him go look at the train tracks for a few minutes, and then we will go into the store." So we walked over to the train tracks, and he was happy to look at them. After a few minutes, I said it was time to go to the store, and I started directing him leave the tracks. This was a disaster.

Daniel went into a full-blown meltdown. He sat down on the ground and refused to come with me. I picked him up and took him into the parking lot near a cart collector outside. I could not physically get him to let me put him into a shopping cart. I could not calm him down. While he was only about 2.5 years old, I was not able to manage him physically to even get him all the way to the store. I had to give up. I struggled to get him back to the car. I was eventually able to buckle him into his car seat.

We went home without stepping foot into the grocery store. This day is a significant memory for me on how unpredictable Daniel's emotions could be, and how helpless I felt in not being able to manage him or conduct basic daily activities because of his difficulty with undesired transitions.

TIP: An effective visual cue Carrie and Jake used for signaling "bedtime" to Daniel was to turn the lights on and off in the room and announce it was bedtime. This was a good cue that gave Daniel a repeatable routine, once it was established. This simple action helped him begin making the transition from playtime to bedtime.

TIP: To demonstrate the passage of time, like "5 minutes", you can utilize a visual timer. Carrie and Jake used this tool heavily with Daniel. It is a great visual indicator for a child to reference. You can tell your child: "When the red section is all gone, then all done trains." "When the red is all gone, you can play cars". Or, "When the sand is all down, all done food." You can use it for communicating any upcoming transition. A couple illustrations of types of visual timers are just after these tips.

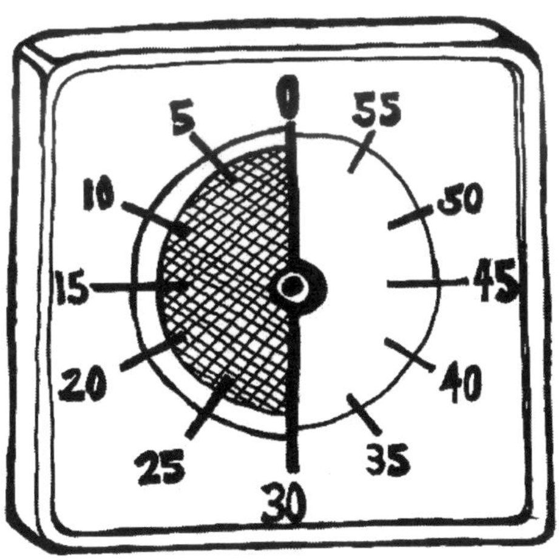

- **Anxiety, Obsessive Compulsive Disorder (OCD), and Depression Challenges**

Casi (Clinician): Along with the autism diagnosis, it is important to understand that sometimes symptoms of other disorders are present, but may not indicate the need for a separate diagnosis. Instead, the approach is behavioral, but in a modified way. There are a lot of individuals with an ASD diagnosis that have anxiety related behaviors, have symptoms of depression, or suffer from OCD tendencies. The crucial component to addressing these behaviors is to understand what is causing the specific behavior (Autism's Associated Medical and Mental-Health Conditions, 2017). This will then inform you how to help!

When symptoms of disorders, separate from autism, are present, the necessary steps to take can be unknown. For anxiety, baby steps need to be taken. With depression in older children, it's about helping them gain awareness of what their body signals are, increase their emotional vocabulary and insight into what is causing them to feel so down, but in a very direct, logical way. With OCD tendencies, it's working on their flexibility, while providing them with coping mechanisms during the times where they would normally want to engage in that behavior. The bottom line is that sometimes the characteristics related to these "co-morbid" disorders are simply a part of the ASD diagnosis, and sometimes they need further treatment by a provider who specializes in that specific disorder.

Similarly, it is important that when you see symptoms of these other challenges happening in your child, you seek help. Some providers are capable and willing to target behaviors in a different way, according to the other disorder symptoms present, while others are not. Find the one that fits your child.

For example, Daniel had anxiety about wearing different shoes. He had the ability to wear different shoes because there was no difference in how they felt on his feet; however, he had made a rule (rigidity) about only wearing a specific type of shoe and nothing different. To help him through this, we slowly desensitized him to wearing only one shoe and instead got him used to new shoes. This strategy is different than merely shoving new shoes onto his feet and making him withstand it, because it takes his anxiety into account. The reason it is important to take his anxiety into account is because his anxiety has different behavioral underpinnings than an avoidant or attention seeking behavioral function. With an attention seeking or avoidant function of behavior, the solution would be to ignore the behavior you don't like and require the child to follow through with the demand. An anxiety function adds an entirely new and complex layer of behavior. If we were to respond to Daniel's shoe preference with a follow through type response by forcing the shoes on him, this would increase his anxiety and therefore make the behavior worse and eliminate any teachable moment, rather than getting him "used to" the new shoes.

Carrie (Mother): Casi has helped me learn that children with autism often grow up to be adults with autism who also are prone to anxiety, OCD, and depression.

After Daniel's diagnosis, while we were still receiving birth-to-three early intervention services, I started to notice that Daniel would get very stressed out and upset about losing things. One of the first examples I remember of this, specifically, was after a session heading out to the parking lot with Daniel. I had some pumpkin seeds in a bowl for him and it got knocked around as I was trying to get him in his car seat. So some of the pumpkin seeds fell onto the parking lot pavement; but not all of them. There were still a lot of seeds he could still eat. However, he looked at those seeds on the ground as if he had just lost his best friend. He got very upset, to a degree that I thought was quite unusual. I just noted it, but then several other examples of this type of concern started arising.

Another key example I remember is when I put some strawberries on a plate for Daniel. He was having trouble eating them, in the sense that he wasn't eating them. But I knew he liked strawberries. He wanted to hold the whole container from the grocery store (the plastic container that a batch of strawberries comes in). So, I put the bin on the table by the plate of strawberries I'd prepared for him, and then he ate the strawberries on the plate. Interesting.

Another similar example was with a chocolate cupcake. When Daniel was about 3.5 years old, I found a gluten-free, dairy-free brand of chocolate cupcake. I would give him a cupcake, but he would get upset after starting to eat it. He loved chocolate cake and wanted to eat the cupcake, but he would start and then stop. Through trial and error, I finally figured out that if I put a "perfect" uneaten cupcake on a separate plate on the table and then gave him a cupcake to eat, he would be able to eat the cupcake in front of him…even if it crumbled. We figured out that he needed this "model" to reference as he ate his portion.

What was interesting to me about Daniel's reaction was that it was as if Daniel would truly grieve the disruption to the perfection of whatever it was that he was "missing" or that he was "losing". It wasn't about him just not getting his way. A bowl of strawberries, pumpkin seeds, the cupcake…in each of these examples, he was truly grieving their loss of perfection; and it was if it hurt him to be in the presence of that imperfect item.

One thing we started doing (per Casi's advice) was to break a cookie into bites so that he could get a snack he loved, but in an imperfect form. We worked to build a tolerance in Daniel to this. He hated the cookie bites at first, and he would cry over them. We had to restrict access to "whole" cookies. He definitely still wanted a cookie as a treat, but he just didn't want it served in bites. When we told him that the bites were how he was going to get the cookie, he eventually accepted them. However, I had to be careful not to let him see me break up the cookie into bites. If he saw me with the original whole cookie, and then saw me dismantle it, this would send Daniel into a meltdown. We kept restricting access to the whole cookie and practiced with him to accept the bites.

Whole Cookie

Cookie Bites

Additionally, when Daniel would experience the loss of a particular food or toy, he was not easily satisfied with a replacement. I can specifically remember an instance of this when Daniel was 4 years, 2 months old. We were driving on our way home from a family road trip. I was giving Daniel one of his preferred treats: a gumdrop type of candy. As I handed the gumdrop to him, he didn't grasp it well enough and it fell down onto the seat below his car seat. I couldn't reach it from the front seat, but I had more gumdrops. So, I tried to give him a different (new) gumdrop. However, he would have nothing to do with my new offer. He wanted the original gumdrop still down in the seat. In situations like this, replacements were not good enough. He would grieve the original lost piece of popcorn, gumdrop, or whatever it might be.

Even when Daniel was over 5 years old, I continued to see examples where Daniel faced concerns about loss of wholeness and simply loss of things he likes. He often drank chocolate milk before bed. There were times where he would drink all of the milk with no problem. But then there were other times where he would leave a little bit in the bottom of the cup and then ask for more milk. I would tell him "but you still have some left in your cup." And he said in a sad way, "I know, but if I drink it, it will be all gone." Hmm. Interesting.

In my examples I listed above, I had to alter my mindset. If I were to get angry with Daniel because he was "wasting" the cupcake he took one bite of and then didn't want anymore, I would miss the whole construct of what was going on in his thought process. I'm not going to punish him and give him a lecture for not appreciating that the cupcake cost $4.00. I'm not going to give him a timeout for saying he wanted the cupcake so badly (even crying for it) and then rejecting it after one bite. To a "typical" adult dealing with a "typical" child, it would be tempting to think the child is being difficult and "spoiled".

He is not trying to be a "difficult" child by not eating the cupcake or the cookie once it loses its wholeness. Instead, the imperfect cupcake or cookie is a true offense to his perception of the world. He cannot tolerate the imperfect food or toy, once he sees it as imperfect. I need to understand this and then learn ways to help him work through these situations. He will have more success (and less stress) in life if he can learn tools to tolerate the dilemmas presented to him by imperfect items. I can recognize that if we don't teach him tools to adapt, he could grow up not understanding how to adjust to changes and unexpected outcomes.

Another thing we would do (per Casi) to help Daniel release some of his rigidity around loss of wholeness was to purposefully make him "lose" some of his snack. He often eats the gluten-free Kettle Corn popcorn, so we would start with a bowl of it for him as a snack. He might be happily eating it, but then we would spill a bit of it on the table. He might try to put the pieces back in his bowl. Then, Casi would "accidentally" knock a piece or two of popcorn off the table. Daniel would start getting upset and would want the pieces back. Casi would say, "No, it's dirty now, it needs to go in the garbage." This could cause a meltdown, even though he still had plenty of popcorn left in his bowl. We would then work through the meltdown to help him self-regulate. But we would not give the "dirty" popcorn back. It would go in the trash.

TIP: If any behavioral symptom comes up involving depression, anxiety or OCD, Consult a professional who has background in working through these behaviors.

- **Aggression (Impulse Control) Challenges**

Casi (Clinician): For many kids, aggression is a way to get their point across or to communicate their wants and needs. When aggression arises, it is important to understand the reason why this behavior is happening. See Chapter 8, Fundamentals of Behavior. Then, and only then, can you determine the correct way to address it. For example, if a form of aggression is used to gain attention, ignoring the behavior is the best course of action, while protecting yourself or others from danger. If the aggression is due to an inability to communicate wants and needs and therefore is done out of frustration, redirect the aggression and then, after a pause, teach a more appropriate way of obtaining those wants and needs, which is then rewarded. Bottom line:

the reason behind any behavior needs to be determined before any intervention is created and used (Cooper et al, 2007).

Carrie (Mother): Daniel began biting and hitting other children and adults, including Jake and me, when he was about 16-18 months old. This was a big obstacle for me, as a mother. If I had not had a child who was a biter, I know for sure that I would have had some judgment and insensitivity to other parents of biting children. I did not understand it. When Daniel began biting, it made me cringe to think of what other parents would surely think of me. They would think what I would have thought if I were in their shoes, such was why aren't that child's parents doing something to stop the biting? They need to pay more attention. The potential for Daniel to bite another child brought me a lot of stress. I worried about this happening during the day at childcare, and I was very nervous about him being in the nursery at church.

Before we began ABA, if Daniel bit us or hit us or bit another child, we would scold him and tell him not to bite or hit. We would give him timeouts. We would make a big deal of it. As we began work in our ABA sessions, Casi asked us to do our best to not react to any of Daniel's biting or hitting. This was an unusual concept for me. She shared that giving him attention for the biting or the hitting, even though it was negative attention, was still attention. Also, removing him from the situation when he bit (like for a timeout) could actually be giving him what he wanted. Going to a timeout might not have felt like a punishment to a child who prefers not to interact. All of this was counterintuitive to my way of thinking, but we complied. We began to ignore his hitting. We would not scold him when he bit us. We would not respond to his action.

Casi (Clinician): With Daniel's biting, there were two components: frustration and communication, and I did not want to add an attention component to it. I provided Jake and Carrie with instruction on how to ignore this type of aggression. The goal was to teach Daniel that communicating his emotions got him faster results than biting us to communicate. I also incorporated self-calming strategies to help him cope with frustrating or overwhelming moments. This approach is not always the way to intervene on such behaviors, which is why it is so important for a qualified therapist to determine the reason for the behavior before an intervention plan is put into place. This will help the child get his/her needs met in a safe way. Always consult a professional when determining the function of a behavior and creating its action plan.

> Tip: When the child pushes, hits, or bites, ignore the behavior and begin to determine the reason it's there in the first place. Redirect the child to different activity. Note: This is much easier said than done, but the rewards and progression are worth the restraint you must show.

- **Self-Injurious Behavior (SIB) Challenges**

Casi (Clinician): Aggression and self-injurious behavior incorrectly get lumped into one category, but in fact they are two very different types of behaviors. Self-injurious behavior is something that shouldn't be taken lightly. This type of behavior is common in children with autism (Minshawi et al, 2014). It doesn't always happen, but when it does, it takes observation and a plan of action to be sure the intervention is addressing the behavior in a way that does not cause the child to increase his/her self-injurious behavior or harm themselves even more. At times, self-injurious behavior can be seen as more harmful than, and a step beyond, aggression towards others. This behavior can have reasons that provide an internal release or sensory satisfaction or it can serve as a 'next step' in an avoidant or attention seeking function of behavior.

For those children that get an internal need met through self-injurious behavior, an intervention plan will address how to stop them from hurting themselves and try to find a mutually exclusive replacement behavior to serve the sensory need. What does this mean? When a person inflicts intentional harm on themselves, it provides them with an automatic sensory reinforcement. Say...what? How can that behavior be reinforcement? Causing pain to themselves is a way to satisfy some sort of need, maybe to get frustration out, or to communicate they are upset. It is an action that will stop when the individual no longer receives the rewards for the behavior. How do we teach an individual that what they feel is not good, when they are the only ones who feel it? This is where the hunt for a replacement behavior is important. (Cooper et al, 2007).

For Daniel, self-injurious behavior occurred in an attention-seeking fashion, as a way to take is behaviors to the next level to see if it would get what he wanted (Cooper et al, 2007). Some of the behaviors Daniel did as a part of this attention seeking progression was head banging, hitting and biting his parents. When attention was not given, he began head banging, but would stop to look to see if Mom and Dad were looking at him injuring himself. He also showed a level of pain awareness as a result of the head banging. With this information, we concluded as a team that he was upping the ante, shifting from hitting and biting others to hitting himself in an attempt to "make" his parents respond. We placed barriers between his head and the hard surface to ensure no notable harm nor damage was occurring to his head and continued ignoring his behavior. After a few more attempts, this behavior ceased (Cooper et al, 2007).

Although in Daniel's case a simple barrier was successful in stopping the behavior from re-occurring, this is not the case for all children. Daniel's example is in no way a guide for how to handle a child who wants to injure himself or herself. With self-injurious behavior, it is essential to make sure you create proper intervention plans as soon as possible so no harm is done to the child. The same is true for the reasons behind SIB. A trained clinician with experience in treating SIB should always be consulted when dealing with this type of behavior.

Carrie (Mother): As Casi describes above, Daniel began hitting himself to heighten the behavior. A majority of the time when he did this, he would slap himself on the top of his nose. He also would sometimes kick the wall very hard. And occasionally, but less often, he did hit his head against a wall. The triggers would occur when he did not get his way. I find this progression fascinating and saddening. But Casi was prepared for this new development.

Casi explained that Daniel's transition from hitting others to injuring himself was essentially him "upping the ante" in his attempt to get his needs or desires met. When we placed demands on him that he didn't want to comply with, he would begin this self-injurious behavior (SIB) where he had previously lashed out at others by biting or hitting.

When he realized that we were no longer responding to the biting and hitting, he changed his response to this self-injurious behavior.

Casi encouraged us to continue not responding to this behavior in a way that Daniel could sense. It is painful to see your child try to hurt himself. This was one area in which I had to harden myself for the end-game potential of Daniel's ultimate positive progress. I remember Casi telling us that we needed to continue to follow through. She reassured us that if Daniel eventually realized that this level of self-injurious behavior would not influence us to release demands on him, then he would eventually stop the SIB.

Another aspect about SIB is that I would read about children going through horrible tantrums, to the point of hitting their heads on the floor repeatedly until they were bleeding, not stopping even then. In some children, it's as if they do not feel the hurt they are inflicting. This high tolerance to pain is another fascinating aspect of some children with autism. However, Daniel did feel pain, and would cry when he got hurt. I was thankful that his SIB was short-lived as we continued to follow Casi's instructions.

It was so amazing when Daniel finally reduced his tendencies to bite others, hit others, and hurt himself.

Chapter Summary:

- This list of behavioral challenges is not exhaustive.
- Children with an autism diagnosis may have their own unique mix of behavioral challenges.
- We provide the information in this chapter, like in the rest of the book, only to help guide you toward acquiring the right type of services for your child. Our strong recommendation, above all other recommendations, is to consult a qualified therapist for addressing your child's specific challenges.

Chapter 10:
Addressing Important Life Skills

Casi (Clinician): We have talked about many different challenges you might face throughout your journey through autism. However, there are some concerns and challenges in areas that are related to life, in general. Below, I cover three major topics, which I address frequently in my work with families: eating challenges, potty training challenges, and bedtime routine challenges. My hope is that you find my experiences and insights helpful.

- **Eating Challenges**

Casi (Clinician): Once of the many challenges parents face with their children is eating or food issues. This is one of the most common obstacles to go through as a parent, especially with a child with autism. The reason this is so frequent is that, for many children, taste, texture and the smell of certain food creates an aversion to it. In addition, many of them have also created "rules" around what foods to eat and not eat. This can be very challenging to parents, as most of the child's preferred foods are not rich in dietary nutrition. And, it is difficult to have any flexibility in place or type of food the family is eating. In fact, most parents of children who have eating challenges due to inflexibility feel as though they are a short order cook, always cooking up something different every night. When this occurs, determine if there is a sensory component to the aversion or if it is more behavioral in nature.

If it is sensory related, professionals such as occupational therapists with specialized training in eating or nutritionists trained in sensory related concerns can address these challenges. If there are other foods within the same sensory category that the child eats, this indicates they do not want to eat that specific food Developing a behavior modification plan utilizing "First/Then" language, rewards, and systematic presentation of the desired food to get them to try and eventually eat the foods you want them to eat is an option (Cooper et al, 2007). Most importantly, consulting with a professional to help you and support you in the process can be beneficial!

TIP: Never assume you know the reason why the child will not eat a specific food. You need to determine the cause for the aversion first, before you begin any food plan. AND, there needs to be reward(s) present to encourage the child to eat the food! Consult a therapist on eating challenges.

- **Potty Training Challenges**

Casi (Clinician): Potty Training is a subject that I LOVE to talk about! The reason is because you can see the connection being made between what a child's body is telling them to do and them controlling their behavior in response to that internal signal. In my opinion, for children with autism, providing potty training in an intensive, clear, systematic manner can be extremely successful. The reason is because the expectations, consequences, and rewards are so clear, leaving minimal uncertainty with what their expectations are.

I typically start with a pre-determined amount of time, usually three to four days, where parents and kids are off of school and work. During this time, we focus solely on potty training and nothing more. This eliminates any extra frustration with other skills or behaviors that are currently being worked on or taught, and the child is able to focus on the contingencies involved with potty training. Typically, after the initial potty training extravaganza, children are able to hold it in between trips to the bathroom, meaning they are they are "trip trained" (Baker & Brightman, 2003; Rogers & Dawson, 2009).

Some challenges that I have worked on with children include bowel movements, going out in public after the initial 3 days of "in the house" potty training,, and how to deal with accidents and initiation after being "trip trained." Since all of these challenges have solutions that are 100% individualized, I cannot give any general advice except to follow through with whatever plan you have developed. The worst thing you can do is start potty training and then back out as soon as there are hiccups. My rule is that once you start, you are in it for the long haul. Also, once underwear is introduced naptime and night time are the only circumstances where a diaper reappears in the picture (Baker & Brightman, 2003). The best thing you can do is get as much support as you can!

TIP: Do not start potty training unless you are ready for it! Be prepared, and get help and support!! It is more about how prepared the parents are and less about the child's readiness. It is all about making a plan and following through with it.

- **Bedtime Challenges**

Casi (Clinician): Bedtime can be a huge time of struggle for some families. For children with autism, the reason can be a lot of different things. Some children have great difficulty sleeping because of internal and biological imbalances. The child's doctor should always be consulted if difficulty staying asleep, once asleep, is the issue.

If the issue is getting to sleep, I have found that adding structure and routines to bedtime consistently every night is helpful. I have also used stories to help the child understand the reason going to bed is a 'must do.' The bottom line is that whether you use music, a special book, object, or even a dance, it should be consistent, every night, at the same time. That will help the child get used to winding down for the day. The expectations need to be clear and just like follow through is important to ABA, it is also important in any other situation for the child. A common thing I tell my parents is that once you decide on a routine or structure, or make a rule about bedtime, stick with it. For example, if bedtime is set for 8:00pm, the child needs to be in bed ready to sleep at 8:00pm. If there are changes to the routine, the child will not truly understand the expectations and therefore have difficulty learning the routine (Cooper et al, 2007).

Chapter Summary

- When working on eating issues, it is important to understand what is causing the child to not eat the food

- Once potty training has started, it is important to keep going to avoid confusion for the child.

- Following through with the bedtime routine will help the child understand your expectations.

Chapter 11:
Will Dietary Changes Help My Child?

Carrie (Mother): A discussion I had with Daniel's new childcare center director prompted me to consider changing Daniel's diet. On the Monday after Daniel's autism diagnosis, I called the new childcare center to confirm they would still accept Daniel to their childcare program now that he had this diagnosis. I spoke with the director. Before answering my question, she started telling me that with diet and exercise, some children with autism can show an improvement in their symptoms. That all sounded nice, but I just really needed to know if she would still take my son into her childcare system. She said she would still accept him as a student at the childcare center, and that was pretty much the end of the phone conversation. I felt relieved because I was juggling work, and I needed to know that Daniel's childcare arrangements were solid.

To my surprise, this childcare director did something else. She followed up that day with an email, and sent me a link to the diet that she had mentioned. I was curious and followed the link. I found an online reference that explained how the gastro-intestinal tract can influence the brain and autism behaviors. In reading this single reference as a starting point, our lives changed that night. Our relationship with autism and food changed that night.

- **My Confusion About the Role of Diet in Daniel's Autism**

Carrie (Mother): At this time, my emotions were frayed. I was still grappling with the reality of the diagnosis. I didn't understand what life would look like going forward and I was worried my son would not become who God intended him to be. Had his natural course always been autism? I just didn't believe that, for him. Was this really just a developmental disorder that was out of our control? Then, why were there reports of early intervention (behavioral and dietary) making a positive difference? Was Daniel's potential future derailed because of his genetics or environment? Could diet really change something going on in his brain? How? Why was I learning about this new nutritional information from Daniel's childcare provider and not from Daniel's doctors? What is going on?

- **My Eyes Were Opened to the Brain-Body Connection**

Carrie (Mother): The childcare center director sent me a link to an online article describing the pathway a child can go down which leads to autism. When I read this brochure, it was very compelling to me. I saw similarities to Daniel's life described in a single page covering a history of ear infections and the use of antibiotics. Then, I read that if you tried the diet, you could start seeing improvement in behavioral symptoms within 10 days. 10 days? Are you kidding? I can do anything for 10 days!

This and other sources note that many children within ASD also have gastro-intestinal difficulties such as chronic diarrhea or constipation, loose bowels, or other types of irregularities. Why is it that people with autism also commonly have digestive disorders, too? Could it be that the developmental disorder is connected to the biological system? This new perspective was fascinating to me. Daniel's diet was something I could control. In a situation where the diagnosis felt like a dead end, and something completely out of my control, I was eager for something active I could do to try to help Daniel.

With this new information, I emailed both the PHD who diagnosed Daniel and Daniel's pediatrician to inform them I wanted to start a gluten-free, dairy-free diet. I wanted permission. Basically, they both responded that changing Daniel's diet would not hurt him, but that I shouldn't get my hopes up. With Daniel's current medical team informed, I decided to try some dietary changes. This was all before I met Casi (but only a few weeks, if not days, before I met her).

When we began the dietary changes, I didn't exactly know what to expect. However, the research I did shared these timeframes for elimination of dairy and gluten.

- Dairy takes approximately three days to leave the system (McCandless, 2009).
- Gluten takes up to eight months for gluten to clear from the system (McCandless, 2009).

As I started the dietary changes, I attributed most of Daniel's early behavioral improvements to dairy removal, knowing that it might take longer for the positive effects of gluten elimination to show up.

Here are some of the positive changes we noticed (and were thrilled by) in the first two months after starting Daniel on a gluten free, dairy free, low soy, low sugar diet:

1) He became more alert (the day we stopped dairy).
2) The long-term exema around his eyes was replaced by beautiful skin (within 4 days of stopping apple juice).
3) He began sleeping through the night (…and I mean all the way through the night).
4) His began more verbal imitation (two days after we stopped dairy).
5) His eye contact improved.
6) He exhibited slight gluten withdrawal symptoms. I saw this as a good sign.
7) His body started presenting new sensitivities; specifically, a reaction to his generic diapers. I interpreted this as part of a detoxification process.

Sounds pretty good, right? It was amazing to see these changes in Daniel, literally all within 2 months of his diagnosis.

- **Information about Autism's Connection to Diet**

Carrie (Mother): There are a few key sources I found which changed my outlook and gave me something I could control with Daniel's new situation as a child diagnosed with ASD. First, the Body Ecology Diet's online brochure outlines how a child's autistic behaviors might be associated with dietary challenges (Gates, 2017). Second, the book, Breaking the Vicious Cycle, has an entire chapter dedicated to "The Autism Connection". Third, the best book I learned from regarding dietary changes was Children with Starving Brains. Review Chapter 2 "Gastrointestinal Pathology", Chapter 5 "Gastrointestinal Healing", and Chapter 6 :Feeding the Starving Brain". Fourth, you can also find great ideas and child profiles in Recovering Autistic Children. Start with Chapter 3: "What I Would Do If I were a Parent of an Autistic Child: Recommendations Based on 25 Years of Research Experience." Each of these resources is listed in our references at the back of the book in full detail.

- **Daniel's Health History and Why I Became Optimistic About Dietary Changes**

Carrie (Mother): Daniel was on many rounds of antibiotics as an infant and young toddler due to recurring ear infections. He was 5 months old when he got his first ear infection. These ear infections continued almost back-to-back until he was 9 months old. We then went through a few months without ear infections, but they started up again around 13 months of age. At that point, we scheduled him to get ear tubes. He received tubes at 18 months of age, and that put an end to the ear infections, thankfully. However, The Body Ecology Diet & Autism theory outlined by Donna Gates taught me that the antibiotics could have been harmful to his gut over that period of continuous ear infections.

My first dietary change decision was to reduce Daniel's sugar intake by eliminating apple juice from his diet. This decision happened two days after Daniel's autism diagnosis. Within 4 days after stopping the apple juice, the exema around Daniel's eyes was almost completely clear. Restriction of apple juice was the only change we made in Daniel's diet during those few days. This was my first tangible sign that Daniel was experiencing an abnormal relationship with food that I needed to explore much more deeply.

Encouraged by this quick response to a reduction in sugar, I pursued more changes to Daniel's diet following initial guidance from The Body Ecology Diet information. I stopped dairy milk, and worked to eliminate other forms of dairy. I also started learning about gluten free foods and worked to eliminate all forms of gluten from Daniel's diet.

It took me about two months to get to the point where I more confidently considered Daniel off gluten and dairy (casein). Overall, we pursued a Gluten Free/Casein Free (GFCF), Low Sugar, Low Soy diet. While we try to eliminate soy, I've found it's very difficult to cut out sugar and soy altogether.

- **Pursuit of Blood Tests, Gene Tests and Nutritional Tests (Rule in and Rule Out Process)**

Carrie (Mother): With the initial positive changes I saw in Daniel after pulling back on sugar and dairy (improved eye contact, improved speech, and exema improvement), I felt I might be going overboard with the gluten removal. Maybe I was wasting effort with the gluten-free piece? Maybe I was too paranoid? Could there really be more dietary issues going on that were related to Daniel's autism diagnosis? I was anxious that I might be taking things too far, by pursuing the gluten elimination.

Seeing Daniel's positive behavior and health changes after introducing the GFCF diet, I pursued some rounds of testing for him. These tests included a blood sample panel, a stool sample panel, and a human leukocyte antigen (HLA) gene test. The blood test was intended to test for any abnormal levels. The stool sample was intended to test for normal or abnormal immune system (antibody) response to particular irritants (McCandless, 2009). The stool test also tested for levels of fecal fat which can be an indicator of malabsorption of nutrients (McCandless, 2009). And, the HLA gene panel was to test for gene presence of genes linked to celiac disease and gluten sensitivity (HLA-DQB1 Gene, 2017).

Without sharing Daniel's particular test results, I am thankful for the information we learned from these tests. The information was helpful in my efforts to further rule in or rule out problematic factors for Daniel. Please note that both the stool and gene tests were "home" tests, and I acknowledge that they may not approved by the U.S. Food and Drug Administration. However, I am still thankful for the opportunity to have access to these tests.

- **Malabsorption – An Invisible Villain**

Carrie (Mother): Malabsorption is something I learned more about in the book Children with Starving Brains. Malabsorption is an invisible villain that you may not know is present; so even if a child is eating decent food, he may not be getting all of the available nutrients from it (McCandless, 2009). Daniel was not on a self-restricting diet of only chicken nuggets and peanut butter, as you may experience or read of children with autism. He was a good eater; much better than some other kids his age that I observed. Based on all the other positive changes resulting from his changed diet, it seemed plausible that he may also suffer from malabsorption. I worked to replenish the nutrients his brain needed, and also heal his gut. I pursued dietary changes and supplementation to impact nutrient absorption and intestinal health.

- **My Multi-Faceted Approach in Combatting Autism**

Carrie (Mother): Without purposefully meaning to do so, I essentially implemented my own regimen for Daniel based on a lot of reading and discussion with Daniel's caregivers. This regimen came about as a result of collecting information from different professionals, published sources, and the particular tests mentioned already. Based on all of this combined information, Jake and I shaped an approach for Daniel that included behavioral therapy and nutritional interventions, which I describe in this chapter. I tried to do everything that might be helpful to Daniel's process of escaping autism's hold.

Below is a table outlining the multi-faceted approach we implemented with Daniel.

Intervention	Challenge Addressed	Desired Result
Behavioral Therapy, Speech Therapy, Occupational Therapy	• Behavioral Challenges • Communication Challenges • Learning Challenges	• Teaching more effective communication skills • Teaching independence addressing variety of behavioral challenges • Improved life skills
Probiotics (McCandless, 2009; Seroussi, 2002)	• Gut Damage • Yeast Overgrowth • Loose Stools/Leaky Gut	• Gut Healing • Yeast Crowding Out • Normal Stools • Improved immune system
Supplementation (McCandless, 2009)	• Malabsorption • Self-Restricted Diets	• Improved nutrient absorption • Improved cognitive function • Increased Sleep Duration
Dietary Restriction (McCandless, 2009; Gottschall, 2010)	• Gut Damage • Protecting the Brain from foreign proteins (gluten and casein) • Genetic Predispositions (identified or unidentified)	• Gut Healing • Improved Brain Function • Improved Immune System • Protecting the Brain; Combating Genetic Predispositions that may yet be unidentified • Increased Sleep Duration
Brain Balance Therapy via Chiropractor (Melillo, 2010)	• Behavioral Challenges associated with the brain's right frontal lobe	• New brain connections in the right side of the brain, by stimulating the left side of the body.

- **Not Pretending I'm a Doctor**

Carrie (Mother): As Casi and I discuss in Chapter 12, Navigating the Health Care System, there are a variety of opinions on what therapies and treatments are effective for children with autism, but there is truly no "silver bullet". Because of the lack of a silver bullet, you, as the parent, are ultimately responsible for choosing what therapies and treatment you implement for your child. You are responsible. As a result, you may feel like you are putting together a "recipe" of services or treatments for your child with a variety of professional and parental inputs. Please less involved with your particular situation might criticize your efforts. They may subtly (or not so subtly) accuse you of "playing doctor" with your child if you subscribe to more than one type of treatment.

My suggestion is to ask any person who jokes with you about "playing doctor" what their alternative suggestions might be. What would they do differently? What is their opinion based on? Do they have experience with a child with autism? If they give you solid information and truly have a basis for their advice, then that is wonderful. Maybe you can learn some great information from them. Maybe you have a new ally in this battle against autism. However, if they roll their eyes at your questions and have no new information to share, then I suggest ending the conversation politely and not having that person be part of your inner circle related to selecting care for your child.

Keep moving forward. However, my caution is to continue to ask yourself if you are putting your child in harm's way. Seek trusted counsel on the treatments you are implementing. I continued to ask myself, professionals, and other parents these questions, as well.

Here are some reasons why I don't feel like I tried to be the doctor:

- I kept my medical providers informed of the interventions we were implementing with Daniel.
- I sought the medical opinion about the safety of dietary changes.
- My dietary changes were not extreme. Even with the elimination of gluten and dairy, we still offered Daniel a wide variety of food types.

- I was not changing doses of prescription medications, or using certain medications for off-label purposes.
- I journaled about the changes seen in Daniel.
- I ran professional tests on Daniel's blood and stool to rule in (and rule out) possible treatments for Daniel.
- I continued behavioral therapy, speech therapy, and occupational for Daniel without trying to have dietary changes be the only form of intervention for Daniel.

- **Daniel's Health Seemed to Be at a Tipping Point**

Carrie (Mother): I believe I caught Daniel at a tipping point. If we had not intervened or corrected some natural (or unnatural) processes going on inside of him, then he may have continued on his negative feedback spiral, resulting in deeper impact on his ASD behaviors. I do believe that the gluten free, casein (dairy) free (GFCF) diet played a major role in keeping autism from an increasingly tighter hold on Daniel. When I first learned about the GFCF diet, I was quite unprepared. I felt (and still feel) inadequate, as a cook. I would walk through grocery stores and find GFCF items my son could eat, amazed to discover these new options for him. These options were just sitting there, ready for me to provide to him without needing to spend hours in the kitchen. I would literally be in tears, choked up and prayerfully thanking all the people who had already worked so hard to get these types of foods on the shelves for people like me to buy. I am so thankful.

- **Gap Between Specialties in Physical Health and Mental Health**

Carrie (Mother): As I have sought a variety of services for Daniel including therapy and biological treatments, my experiences with medical professionals have helped me realize how I as the parent must act as the bridge connecting Daniel's various services. This is because medical doctors primarily focus on treating physical ailments. And, psychologists and behavior therapists focus primarily on mental and learning challenges. Of course, this is obvious to you as I write this.

However, because of these specialists' professional focus areas, your child's medical doctors may not seem eager to learn about all that you are doing in your behavior therapy with your child. Comparatively, your child's psychology specialists may not seem overly enthusiastic about new dietary or other biological treatments you might introduce. These non-reactions certainly don't mean that the specialists don't care what you are doing, but they have their defined roles, and they stick within them.

However, what if there is a connection between the physical ailment and the mental challenges? Who is willing to look at both simultaneously? What if you, like I did, notice an undeniable positive change in your child's behavior when you start making nutritional changes or other biological changes? Who else is willing to acknowledge the connection between the brain and the gut? Answer: a lot of people. While certain specialists may not cross over particular subject matter boundaries or entertain the connection between the brain and the body, there are many practitioners and resources that can help you explore this potential connection.

1) Published Resources (Books, Websites):
2) Naturopathic Doctors and Nurses
3) Reputable Sources for Supplements
4) Other Parents
5) Childcare Providers
6) Chiropractors utilizing Brain Balance Therapies (Melillo, 2010)

To be clear, I am not recommending that you do not have medical doctors and psychology specialists on your child's team. However, you do have the option of seeking additional information or involvement from other specialists as part of your effort to incorporate appropriate services and treatments for your child's specific needs.

- **Considering Dietary Changes or Supplementation**

Carrie (Mother): I encourage parents of children with ASD to take a hard look at what might be causing any gastrointestinal difficulties in their child. These observations in my own son have proven to me that the gut-brain connection is real. Improvement in the digestive tract may lead to improvement in behavior and autism symptoms, depending on your child's situation.

Repeating my original questions: Why is it that people with autism also commonly have digestive disorders, too? Could it be that the developmental disorder is connected to the biological component within us? I believe that the answer is yes, based on my experience with Daniel. It is important to ask questions about how gastrointestinal difficulties could be influencing the brain or the immune system's inability to function properly (Gottschall, 2010; McCandless, 2009).

Casi (Clinician): While Daniel and other children respond well to diet and nutrition changes, there are some kids who do not. The research on diets as a treatment for children with ASD is not conclusive. With that being said, I have professionally seen the differences in children who do have gastrointestinal trouble and who have tried certain diets. Specific positive outcomes that some families have experienced include positive changes in behavior, increase in communication and attention, and heightened social awareness and interaction. Throughout my many years in the field I have seen numerous children who have benefitted from a change in their diet. There are tests that can measure specific food allergies and intolerances to help guide families in their decision making process and whether or not begin a dietary change.

I do believe that Daniel is a child who is responsive to dietary changes. We observed his skills and behaviors to be positively impacted by the dietary changes. Not all kids/individuals have this positive response. Every child is unique, and will respond in their own individual way. I encourage all my parents to think about the positives and negatives their dietary choices will mean for their family. If they are dedicated to making changes, make the choice, follow through, and see what happens!

Chapter Summary:

- Why is it that people with autism also commonly have digestive disorders, too? Could it be that the mental is connected to the biological? I believe that the answer is yes, based on my experience with Daniel.
- I shaped an approach for Daniel that included Behavioral Therapy and Nutritional Interventions, which I describe in this chapter. I tried to do everything that might be helpful to Daniel in escaping autism's hold on him.
- The initial positive behavioral changes after changing Daniel's diet combined with test results led me to pursue additional dietary supplements to help Daniel on his road toward better gastrointestinal health.

Chapter 12:
Navigating the Health Care System

Carrie (Mother): Upon initial diagnosis, you may quickly find yourself confronted with all sorts of opinions on what you should do next regarding treatment and/or therapy. There may be therapy available, but you are told it is expensive and there are long waiting lists. Or, you are told there's nothing you can do.

Based on my experience, a parent seeking autism-related services can pursue various treatment paths. However, parents may face some new obstacles in pursuing autism treatment, when compared to other medical challenges. What Casi and I hope to do in this book is help you sift through a variety of these treatment options and obstacles so that you can more confidently pursue appropriate treatments for your child.

- **You Will Need to Develop a Point of View**

Carrie (Mother): As you learn about various services offered for children with ASD, you will come across a lot of different philosophies, theories, and approaches to treating children with ASD. You will have to decide which types of treatment to pursue for your child. With other medical conditions, forming a point of view is not usually something that is required of you. If you have a bacterial infection, you take antibiotics. If you have a broken arm, you get a cast. If you have vision problems, you get glasses.

With a disorder such as ASD, it is challenging to know what will be best for your child. Jake and I felt a new requirement to get educated and form a point of view on which services would be best for Daniel.

Forming a point of view on medical care can be a difficult task to fulfill. It can be a new world for a parent. You start exploring, and then deciding, and then taking action. In addition, sometimes, you must defend your point of view. All of this is possible, but it is very different from just filling a prescription at the pharmacy for a medical condition.

Because there are a variety of treatment opinions and theories out there, you will to need gather information and then form your own point of view on what will be most suitable for your child. This point of view will be formed through trial and error as you experience different types of services. No one has all the answers. Moreover, no one knows your child better than you do.

Casi (Clinician): So, I am sure you are asking, "How do I develop my point of view, when this is whole situation is foreign to me?" Well, that is one reason we wanted to write this book: to give you a taste of what could be helpful. We encourage you to take your family, your time, and your goals are for your child into account. The very first question I ask parents is: "What is important to you, and what do you want to see get better?"

If there are many answers, or just one, to that initial question above, this is your starting point. Begin your search for a provider that can help with that initial answer. In my opinion, narrow down the list to the treatments that are supported by research. Once caveat: there may be interventions that you find, that have not been fully researched yet. My suggestion to you is to dig deeper into the treatments. Look at reputable sources that speak to the positives and negatives of the specific treatment you are contemplating. This will help you develop your point of view on what you want out of a treatment, and what you do not want.

- **Seeking Services and Treatment (Public and Private)**

Carrie (Mother): As the parent of a child recently diagnosed with autism, I began learning that there were many different types of treatment and services offerings, ABA Therapy (discrete, precision, naturalistic), and choices in how it is delivered (home setting or clinic setting). Autism services are provided by medical facilities like hospitals and private organizations, with private therapists. There are also many wonderful services that roll up under the state, county, or school district in which you live. How do you find these services?

Casi (Clinician): The hard part about both private and public treatment options is that in some areas, options are limited. So, how do you find services when it seems like there are none available? Answer: talk to your pediatrician, talk to other moms, and talk to schools! Seek out and speak to nonprofit agencies in your area; ones specializing in individuals with disabilities. These organizations may help families find services.

- **Treatment Options**

Carrie (Mother): Upon diagnosis, the psychologist told us that we should pursue Applied Behavioral Analysis (ABA) therapy. ABA is a type of behavioral therapy often recommended for children on the autism spectrum (see Chapter 4, Fundamentals of ABA). As a parent of a newly-diagnosed child, I entered into the world of ABA with very few preconceived opinions, so I was oblivious to the variety of opinions associated with ABA. However, I soon encountered some of the different approaches to ABA. There are different schools of thought on ABA approaches. You will hear the terms "precision", "discrete", and "naturalistic". You will hear the terms "clinic environment" or "clinic setting" and "home environment". How do you decide which type to begin? How do you seek out different types?

I suggest evaluating the ABA approaches and other treatments in order to start learning more about what might be best for your child. In my view, starting ABA therapy of any type is better than not starting at all. Keep taking action to find the right type of therapy, and the right therapist, for your child. You can continue making adjustments along the way.

In addition to introducing ABA therapy as a treatment for your child, there are other therapies and treatments you can pursue. These additional services and treatments can complement the work done in ABA therapy. Depending on the needs of your child, professionals will likely begin recommending a set of complementary therapies and treatments you can combine as you shape your child's "set" of services. In the previous chapter about dietary changes (Chapter 11, Will Dietary Changes Help My Child?), I outlined the set of services we pursued for Daniel after his diagnosis. The mix of services and treatments Jake and I chose for Daniel will not necessarily be the best mix for your child. I encourage you to seek the services that make the most sense for your child. You can continue to evaluate along the way if your child is responding positively to particular services, and make appropriate decisions to phase in or phase out certain ones.

The book, Recovering Autistic Children, was a key source which helped me start learning about treatment options parents utilize in addition to ABA therapy. It is a compilation of many families' own journeys with autism, where the parents discuss each child's path.

Casi (Clinician): I believe that a behavioral approach should be used to treat autism. Other services may be explored for use in conjunction with an ABA Therapy, but the ABA therapy is good to consider having as a cornerstone to your mix of services.

- **Find a Therapist That's Right for Your Child and Family**

Carrie (Mother): You will soon learn when you make therapy appointments that they will book you with the same therapist all the time, because that therapist will "learn" your child the best, including your child's personality and "triggers". In most therapy environments, you do not get a new therapist every treatment session or you do not see someone different to makeup a session. Therefore, it's very important to get a good therapist, and one that you don't mind seeing a lot.

Casi (Clinician): If the therapist is a good fit with your family, you will not want to switch between different therapists. Otherwise, it may feel like you are going back to square one at every session because there is no continuity of service and treatment styles. The downfall is if something happens with the schedule, or an illness or leave of absence occurs, you will have to weigh the options to see what the appropriate next step will be for your family. A good clinician will talk with you about the options if there is an upcoming period where they need to be absent from therapy, such as a role transition or their own medical leave. Communication is the key to making therapist transitions as smooth as possible, as well as handling any discontent about the frequency of missed visits.

- **Should I Medicate My Child?**

Per the CDC,

> "There are no medications that can cure ASD or treat the core symptoms; however, there are medications that can help some people with ASD function better. To learn more about medications and ASD, visit the Food and Drug Administration's website at www.fda.gov" (CDC Community Report on Autism, 2016, p.39).

Carrie (Mother): To date, Daniel has not received prescribed medication to help control or maintain some of his progress as we address his position on the ASD spectrum. I know that Daniel could be a candidate for some sort of medication in the future. I'm not against medication, but I do like to try other treatment options first.

Casi (Clinician): As a behavior therapist/mental health professional, I am not qualified to prescribe medication, however I will refer my clients to an appropriate professional if the topic of medication comes up. I do think that there are times that when medication can help an associated disorder (such as anxiety, ADHD, OCD). Sometimes this treatment addition can open the windows and doors to behavior change. However, it is my opinion that trying behavioral modifications and interventions can be a helpful first step.

Working with Insurance Providers

Casi (Clinician): From my point of view, it is extremely helpful for parents to advocate for the services you want for your child. Become informed about your specific plan and what your particular carrier will or could provide, and find out those parameters right away. Work with members of your professional team to obtain information on the types of services for which your providers can bill. Become knowledgeable.

Carrie (Mother): As a parent of a child diagnosed autism, I have not developed an expertise on working with insurance providers to optimize quantity services and financial coverage. I know many other parents are much more informed than I on how to navigate the insurance system. Learning more about strategies to maximize insurance coverage is something I would still like to master. However, I have learned a few nuances regarding what treatments and services are covered by health insurance. There are also nuances to the steps you need to take to submit the right information to receive payments.

For example, some insurance carriers provide coverage for ABA services and some do not. Some may specify that services must be in the "clinic" setting rather than the "home" environment. Some types of coverage may limit the number of sessions on a monthly or annual basis. Sometimes coverage will be paid based on certain medical billing codes. Sometimes payment requires your provider to have a certain education degree or certification. Sometimes your provider may require you to submit paperwork to your insurance, rather than them providing that insurance claim submission service.

One enlightenment I had in seeking services that could fit within our budget was that I did not absolutely have to function within the constraints of my insurance plan. In certain cases, you may decide you want to see a particular provider or seek a particular service, for which insurance does not pay. Often, you have the option pay out of pocket for services. This knowledge gave me access to a wider variety of providers or services, but some of these options were a challenge to pursue because of financial constraints.

That's where some creativity, strategy, and prioritization came in for us. Some things I learned and saw other parents do were very helpful. For example, I learned the per-month allowable number of sessions and how to time your appointments in such a way as to obtain maximum insurance coverage. I've seen some parents begin a fundraising effort on behalf of their child. Another way to be creative about your out of pocket expenses is by establishing a home therapy program where you utilize less costly "ABA Consultants" who operate under the direction of your primary behavior therapist. I discuss this process in Chapter 7: Establishing an ABA Home Therapy Program.

- **Keep Moving Forward**

Carrie (Mother): Whatever services and therapies you pursue, try to have confidence that the steps you are taking will lead you forward, not backward. That is the way that our treatments for Daniel arose and evolved. Jake and I kept moving forward, and through that movement, we would learn of new options. We would learn from professionals and other parents, and find ourselves prepared to make new decisions about Daniel's services. For example, below is a series of our steps which helped us form the services mix for Daniel.

1) Daniel's childcare center recommends a consultation from the local early intervention agency (seven months prior to diagnosis).

2) The consultant from the local early intervention agency encouraged us to pursue a developmental evaluation (five months prior to diagnosis).

3) Daniel's pediatrician referred us to a local autism clinic and a private psychologist to pursue an autism diagnostic evaluation (five months prior to diagnosis).

4) Daniel qualified to start receiving speech and occupational therapy from the early intervention program after receiving their comprehensive evaluation (two months prior to diagnosis).

5) We began to understand that the childcare center Daniel attended may not be the best environment for Daniel, given our new knowledge of his needs. We pursued finding a new childcare that would tailor some specific accommodations for Daniel (one month before diagnosis).

6) Daniel received a diagnosis of Autism Spectrum Disorder by the clinical psychologist, who had been referred to us by our pediatrician (day of diagnosis).

7) I researched autism heavily (same month as diagnosis and continuing for subsequent months).

8) We located a new childcare center we felt would better accommodate and address Daniel's challenges. We told the childcare director about the autism diagnosis. The new childcare director told me about the possibility of dietary changes helping the symptoms of children with autism. She also told me about the chiropractor who practiced Brain Balance therapies (Melillo, 2010) (same month as diagnosis).

9) Through my online research, I found a local autism treatment organization. I began learning more about the organization (one month after diagnosis).

10) We pursued dietary changes, with dramatic improvements in Daniel. Primary changes were going gluten free and dairy free, along with adding in some supplements (starting same month as diagnosis).

11) Based on a referral from the private clinical psychologist who diagnosed Daniel, we started ABA therapy with Casi (one month after diagnosis, but continued for approximately three years).

12) We pursued treatment with a chiropractor. The chiropractor helped us learn about brain-based therapies, along with the emotional development related to the brain's right frontal lobe (first 8 months after diagnosis) (Melillo, 2010).

13) Through the local early intervention agency, we received transition information to set us up with our district's special needs preschool (2 months after diagnosis).
    a. The information shared in these sessions helped us understand school district pre-school services and other transition services. The early intervention program helped us know what to expect as we transitioned to the schedule district.

14) We established a home program under Casi's supervision (five months after diagnosis).

15) I found a wonderful ABA consultant to work in Daniel's ABA home program through reviewing the website of the local autism treatment organization's website, where consultants offer up their services. (five months after diagnosis)

16) Because of the success with dietary interventions, I established care for Daniel with a naturopath, along with our original pediatrician (six to twelve months after diagnosis).

17) Through the preschool, I was able to start meeting other parents and invited them and their child over for play dates (six to twelve months after diagnosis).

This journey continues, with similar interactions that lead to learning and new steps.

Chapter Summary:

- Search for clinicians who want to help parents learn their techniques.
- Because there are a variety of treatment opinions and theories out there, you will need gather information and then form your own point of view on what will be most suitable for your child.
- Even with an autism diagnosis, some insurance carriers do not provide full coverage for ABA services or other services that might be helpful.
- Whatever services and therapies you pursue, try to have confidence that the steps you are taking will lead you forward closer to the optimal mix of services for your child.

Chapter 13:
Working with Local Services and Schools

- **From a Legislative Point of View, Your Child has Rights**

Carrie (Mother): This chapter will not be an exhaustive review of the education system and disability resources in the United States, but Casi and I would like to share a few key things you may find helpful. The first part of this chapter reviews some general education regulation terms, and then I will share more of my own experience of navigating the county services, school district services, and private services. We have listed out some a quick reference list of education terms and acronyms at the end of this chapter.

One of the best sources I have found that explains your child's rights to evaluation, treatment and education is a 2015 Clinical Report from the American Academy of Pediatrics (AAP). It covers the services available nationally due to federal regulation. I highly recommend you review it, regardless of your stage in your journey. The Clinical Report is entitled "The Individual With Disabilities Education Act (IDEA) for Children With Special Education Needs," authored by Paul H. Lipkin, Jeffrey Okamoto and the COUNCIL ON CHILDREN WITH DISABILITIES and COUNCIL ON SCHOOL HEALTH.

- **Introduction to Terms and Sources for Education Information**

Carrie (Mother): Some terms you will encounter within the public education and public health systems are below, all of which are referenced in the AAP 2015 Clinical Report noted above (Lipkin et al, 2015).

- EI: Early Intervention
- FAPE: Free and Appropriate Public Education (1975)
- IDEA: Individuals with Disabilities Education Act
- IDEA Part A: General Provisions for IDEA
- IDEA Part B: Guidelines for Ages 3-21 years
- IDEA Part C: Guidelines for Ages 0 up to 3 years (Birth to 3 Services)

- Child Find: As part of IDEA Part C, your local area likely also has services to help identify pre-K children who may be exhibiting developmental delays (Lipkin et al, 2015).
- IEP: Individualized Education Program.
- IFSP: Individualized Family Service Plan
- LRE: Least Restrictive Environment

Local Services

- **Early Intervention Agency Programs**

Carrie (Mother): You likely have an early intervention services provided by the early intervention agency in your community, as it is a federally funded program. Look for these services! Our local early intervention agency enabled us to begin receiving weekly speech therapy and occupational therapy for Daniel in advance of him receiving the autism diagnosis. In Chapter 2, Recognizing a Developmental Delay, I write in depth about our introduction to the local early intervention program and services.

Our local early intervention program included the following steps for the services Daniel received:

1. Initial developmental consultation (at our childcare). The results of this evaluation lead to the recommendation for a full developmental delay evaluation.

2. Full developmental evaluation. The results of this evaluation lead to the recommendation for Daniel to start receiving services from therapists from the early intervention program.

3. Assignment of a Family Resource Coordinator (FRC). This person essentially served as our caseworker within the Birth to Three Services Program.

4. Receipt of the Individualized Family Support Plan (IFSP). This document stated the service plan for Daniel, and what services he was going to receive. This IFSP document is similar to a school district's Individualized Education Plan (IEP), which I will discuss later in this chapter. The IFSP served as nice precursor to receiving our first IEP.

5. Daniel began weekly therapy sessions. For some sessions, we had appointments at the early intervention agency location. However, some of these sessions occurred onsite at Daniel's childcare center. In my view, this accommodation to have the therapist travel to the childcare center is an excellent part of the program. To know that Daniel was receiving a therapy session while Jake and I were at work was such a comfort.

6. Receipt of an IFSP 6 Month Review. This document states progress toward Daniel's established goals.

7. Receipt of Daniel's Exit Report from the Birth to 3 Early Intervention Program, just prior to Daniel's 3rd birthday.

Casi (Clinician): An Individual Family Support Plan (IFSP) is a plan created to help families and school professionals know what the current challenges are for children and families, both in the home and school setting. This is where home-based intervention services, such as birth to three services, are provided in the home to help children and parents learn strategies to help with the progression of skills.

School Districts

- **Transitioning from the Early Intervention Program to Your School District**

Carrie (Mother): Once your child turns three years of age, he will not be eligible for the Birth to 3 services. Your child will need to transition into your school district. As Daniel approached age 3, our local Birth to 3 Services Early Intervention Agency held a series of transition meetings that parents could attend to learn more about transitioning services for our child into our local school district. These information sessions covered pre-school options for the children, given one's current school district.

At these sessions, I started realizing how fortunate it was that we lived in a great school district, which could help us address Daniel's challenges. I began learning that other parents often move in order to get their children services in a desirable school district. I was thankful that we did not have to make big changes like that. I began realizing we were going to be able to get good services for him.

Navigation of the world of special needs services started to make a little more sense. I started to feel like I could lean on something. My knowledge was growing, but there was still so much to learn.

Casi (Clinician): At the time when early services for your child cease, the next step can be very scary and daunting. Are you in a district with adequate school services for your child? Are there schools around you that offer open enrollment? Would you move to a different district? These are all very common and real questions parents ask themselves. I mentioned the idea of open enrollment. This is where you can enroll your child in a neighboring district, at no extra charge. Some districts allow this and some do not.

Carrie (Mother): Your school district may provide a wonderful set of pre-kindergarten services. Check with your Birth to 3 resources and school district websites to learn more about these services. Depending on your child's needs, the school district may establish a customized Individual Education Plan (IEP) that will assure particular services and accommodations are in place for your child.

- **Putting a 3 Year Old on a School Bus**

Jacob (Father): I don't think I will ever forget the moment Daniel and I walked out the door for his first day of preschool and taking the bus to his school. He had his backpack on. He was dressed nicely, and I recall he was excited to ride the bus. But I was a nervous wreck, as well as a proud dad, all in one. My boy was going off to school and taking the bus, nonetheless, for a 30-minute ride each way to his school. He was the first child picked up on the bus route, and had the longest ride. Daniel and I waited outside.

As the bus pulled up, we stepped on and introduced ourselves to the bus driver. I put Daniel in the front seat just behind the door and buckled him in, kissed him goodbye, and away they went. And away I went also, following in my truck close behind that school bus. As the bus made its way through the neighborhoods picking up a dozen or so more kids, I just stopped behind the bus at each stop, hoping and praying that he was not afraid; that he wasn't crying or having a hard time.

This was a big step for both him and us, as parents. For me, it was akin to releasing him into the world and letting go of him for the first time. We had always been Daniel's shelter, safety, and comfort of a parent's touch and sound of our voices. I watched from a distance as the bus pulled up to the school and saw my little hero get off the bus in fine shape, as if he had enjoyed the whole ride. He shuffled into line with the other children, walked into the building, and disappeared through the reflection on the glass doors.

This was Daniel's routine literally every school day morning for the next three years.

All the bus drivers we had were so great with all the kids; always kind and gentle, and they enjoyed driving for the special needs kids. One of my highlights about the bus drivers is about my good friend, who went to our church and was a special needs bus driver in our district. He cared so much about me and my family that he asked to transfer routes so that he could drive Daniel to school every morning in Daniel's last year of preschool.

This is how I knew that a community is needed to help raise, shape and care for your kids when you are not there. This was an awesome expression of loving kindness. This has to be on the top of my list as one of my proudest moments as a father, as Daniel conquered my hurdle for him with ease. And, looking back, maybe it was a foretelling tale of things to come, for him.

- **Transitioning From Pre-School to Kindergarten**

Carrie (Mother): When Daniel started kindergarten, I was amazed and thrilled that two of his main teachers/administrators from the pre-school system were there to help transition the pre-school kids into their kindergarten class. They had previously told me they would check in on Daniel early in this school year, but I did not realize they would be there the first day. It made me feel more comfortable with him making the adjustment to kindergarten by being able to see some familiar teacher faces that first day of kindergarten. Another way to help your child feel more comfortable is to take your child to the school a few times before they actually start there. Help them become familiar with these new surroundings before their first day; even if it's just to the playground outside the school (like in the summer, when the school is locked up).

There are local, private pre-schools that we could have opted for with Daniel to help him prepare for kindergarten. However, I have found so far that there have been many benefits to already having him be "known" by the school district and the teachers. They helped make his transition very smooth.

Casi (Clinician): Transitioning from pre-school to kindergarten is a big step for children and parents! The big question is how is it done so the child is set up to succeed? One way to help ease nerves is to establish a good communication system. This can take the form of a communication log, a notebook, or emails. It is helpful to have a written form of communication so you can go back and look at what the teacher says about your child that week. An effective way to can be through help the school staff understand your child the best they can is to be open about the struggles and achievements your child is showing at home. This will help them "see" your kiddo the way you see him/her, and help the staff understand your point of view. .

- **Skills Needed to Function in a General Education Classroom**

Carrie (Mother): In order for your child to function successfully in a general education classroom, some key skills are required (Lipkin et al, 2015). Two of them are below:

1) Sit at a desk or table for the duration of classes or activities, and
2) Follow the teacher's agenda without causing disruption to their own learning or that of other students

Teachers, of general education classrooms, may not be specifically trained to work with children with special needs. If children (typical or with special needs) are not able to follow along within the controlled environment of the classroom, teachers will not be able to effectively manage their classrooms.

Casi taught me about these two requirements early on in Daniel's ABA therapy, when Jake and I asked her about Daniel's potential to attend kindergarten in a general education school. I'm so thankful for this knowledge. It helped us prioritize the importance of Daniel's therapy, and it gave us a long-term vision for what Daniel was working toward.

Casi (Clinician): The skills Carrie mentions above are directly related to how a child will access their educational environment. One reason to focus on classroom skills and strategies is to increase the child's exposure to the general education setting, or mainstreaming. There are some instances in which a mainstream classroom is not a good fit for a child with autism. It all depends on what extra help they will need, and the areas they need it in. Some questions that can be helpful in figuring out educational placement are: Do they have the necessary social skills to be successful in a general education classroom? Can they complete the "must do's" of school? Will they be able to maintain their engagement on a topic that is not within their interest list? Is the classroom a good fit for them? The child's IEP team, which includes the parents, is in charge of determining the answers to these questions. One of my professional missions is to empower parents to stand up for what is best for their child and work together with the school system to figure out the best option and solution to any academic setting question. Regardless of the decision, it is important for parents to be advocates for their children.

Carrie (Mother): Daniel entered kindergarten with his age group. He is one of the older children in his class because of his autumn birthday. Because of the school district's pre-school program, and Child Find, and Casi, and ABA, and early intervention program services, and dietary changes, Daniel entered kindergarten. Through the school district, he qualifies to have an Individualized Education Plan (IEP).

- **What is an IEP? How Do I Get One For My Child?**

Casi (Clinician): An IEP is a legal document that stipulates, or explains, what services a child receives. This includes the placement for the child, and location these services will be provided in as well as any accommodations and modifications that the child needs throughout his/her day to be successful. To get an IEP, a child needs to be assessed through the school district and found to have areas of difficulty in areas such as speech, occupational therapy, physical therapy or behavioral difficulties. Meeting qualifications in some or all of these areas indicates that the child needs extra services from the school district.

Carrie (Mother): Because we were working with the local Birth to 3 Early Intervention Program prior to Daniel turning 3 years old, we were able to take advantage of the transition program they established. Once Daniel turned three, he would no longer be eligible to receive the Birth to 3 services. The Early Intervention Program helped us phase in to our school district's pre-school services once Daniel turned three years old.

As I wrote about earlier in the book, I attended a couple of transition meetings at our local early intervention agency. These meetings helped us figure out how to work with the school district to get the School District Evaluation scheduled. The school district offered a special needs pre-school program to children starting at age three. With Daniel's birthday in October, we were scheduled for a district evaluation the August before his 3rd birthday. We received an "Initial Individualized Education Program Invitation" (IEP).

- **Setting Goals for the IEP**

Carrie (Mother): Your IEP team will distribute the proposed IEP to you, and they will review the goals they have pulled forward from previous documentation. Additionally, they may introduce new goals for your child. This is also the discussion where you would want to add in your own input for what goals you would like to see included. Decide if you agree with the goals set for your child, and let your support or corrections be known. Below are a couple of the goals established for Daniel's very first IEP in pre-school.

Based on the goals established, and the services for which Daniel qualified, below is the schedule of services Daniel received his first year of pre-school.

- **IEP Meetings with the School District**

Carrie (Mother): During the school year, my experience has been that we have two scheduled IEP meetings per year, unless extra meetings become necessary. I can also request additional meetings. Generally, the resource counselor, or similar role, will contact you to schedule these meetings, and your child's teacher and the other IEP team members will attend the meeting. You will have to provide your signature for each meeting you attend. Everything gets documented, which I see as a positive thing.

Casi (Clinician): For IEP meetings, it can be helpful to set goals surrounding necessary discussion topics. This is to streamline thoughts as well as be sure that all important topics are discussed. This can be planned for in any way that allows for parents and school staff to work together.

Carrie (Mother): Daniel's first progress report involved the observance by his teachers of skills in the categories of "Demonstrates", "Emerging", or "Not Yet".

Daniel primarily scored in the "Not Yet" or "Emerging" category. While this report was another confirmation of Daniel's delays, it was good for me to learn the skills that were appropriate for his age. To see the skills written out this way helped me begin to appreciate the process of early childhood development.

- **What are Some Challenges I Might Face with the School District?**

Casi (Clinician): It is difficult to place challenges with school districts into predetermined categories. Each school district offers a different array of programs and services and also has a variety of resources, staff, and support systems to offer their students. The most important thing you, as parents, can do is to become educated about what system or setup your school district offers or has established. Then, be aware of what your expectations are as a parent regarding where you want your child's placement to be including specific supports and services you think are best for your child. The biggest challenge you may face is that the district does not agree with your viewpoints of best fit placements for your child.

So, how do you handle the situation if both sides do not agree? Answer: In a very calm and diplomatic manner, right from the start. Ideally, you and the school district are on the same team/side, and you want to keep it this way for as long as possible. Try to focus on building the bridge between the school and your family up and still intact.

- **Requesting a Class Visitation from a Private Therapist**

Carrie (Mother): You can request for a therapist or other service provider to observe your child in the classroom setting. Children may exhibit different behaviors in the school and classroom environments than they do while at home. It can be very helpful to learn from this type of observation. Schools generally have a form that you will need to complete to schedule this type of visitation. Also, you may need to be patient with this process, as there are several approval or review steps to go through. If you really want the observation, learn the process and follow it.

TIP: It may be helpful if you already have listed the therapist/consultant as someone to whom the school can release information. Schools generally have release forms for this purpose. Submit this form, and then file the visitation request. Note that you should already have the release form in place when you complete the visitation request.

TIP: Because the school will generally set a date and time window when the visit can occur, I recommend putting the therapist's availability on the visitation request so that you don't have to ask for a rescheduled appointment.

- **What Private Treatment Options are Available?**

Carrie (Mother): Beyond the school district, local resources, and health/hospital Center resources, there were a couple of other private resources that Jake and I came across in our pursuit of services for Daniel. One was a chiropractor referral who focused on brain-based therapies as practiced by Dr. Robert Melillo, author of Disconnected Kids. Another was a referral to a child-directed, relationship-based therapy. Some of the private treatment and therapy services may also qualify for insurance coverage, depending on your insurance plan.

There are also private pre-schools available. Private pre-schools may be a great option for you, depending on your child's needs.

- **Public Schools vs Private Schools: Key Distinction**

Carrie (Mother): Public schools are accountable to uphold IDEA, FAPE, LRE, and IEPs because they receive federal funds. Private schools have no obligation to provide special needs services if they are not receiving federal funding. As a parent, this was a new realization for me. I just always assumed that private schools would provide services above and beyond the public school system. For children with disabilities, this is not always the case. It has been eye-opening for me to learn that Daniel is receiving so many excellent services through his public school system that he would not be entitled to within a private school system.

In the AAP Clinical Review, there is a section that outlines when a child might be placed in a private school to meet the FAPE requirements (Lipkin et al, 2015). However, my understanding is that this would happen only in pretty severe situations.

Casi (Clinician): When thinking about private school, you need to ask the question "Will my child's need be met?" Some private schools do provide options for services for children with special needs. Some even allow you to bring in your own aid to assist your child while in the classroom setting. It is all dependent on the school and their philosophy.

Chapter Summary:

- One of the best sources I have found that explains your child's rights to evaluation, treatment, and education is a 2015 Clinical Report from the American Academy of Pediatrics (AAP). It outlines services available through federal funding, which all states can receive. The Clinical Report reference:

  "The Individual with Disabilities Education Act (IDEA) for Children with Special Education Needs" authored by Lipkin et al.

- Public schools are accountable to uphold IDEA, FAPE, LRE, and IEPs because they receive federal funds. Private schools have no obligation to provide special needs services if they are not receiving federal funding.
- Children may exhibit different behaviors in the school and classroom environments than they do while at home.
- For a child to function successfully in a general education classroom, two key skills he will need are to be able to: 1) sit at a desk or table for the duration of classes or activities, and 2) follow an agenda without disruption to the teacher's schedule (Lipkin et al, 2015).

Chapter 14:
The Decision to Have Another Child

- ## Maybe We Will Just Have One Child

Carrie (Mother): Before Daniel was diagnosed with autism, we had always wanted more than one child. Before I became pregnant with Daniel, I did not suffer a miscarriage. Daniel was my 1st pregnancy, and it went smoothly. I loved being pregnant, and was filled with the anticipation, dreams, stress, and physical changes all mixed together.

We were thinking about a second child as Daniel started going through his initial developmental evaluations at about 22 months of age, before we really knew how serious things were going to get. I actually became pregnant twice before Daniel was diagnosed. One pregnancy ended in a very early miscarriage and one ended because it was a molar pregnancy (look it up if you want to learn more).

Two months after the molar pregnancy ended, Daniel was diagnosed with autism at 28 months. Although I didn't really know it at the time (but learned soon enough), the ending of a molar pregnancy comes with a necessary waiting period afterwards. It would end up putting our 2nd baby plans "on hold" for almost exactly one year. That year of being "on hold" was the most intense year of our learning curve with autism. During this time of Daniel's heavy treatment, we began to adjust to the idea that maybe we would only have one child.

Before my own experiences, I had never really understood why married couples might choose to only have one child. The only reasons that occurred to me were:

1. You had one child at a later age, so there just wasn't time to have another.
2. You didn't have the finances to support another child.
3. Your marriage may not have survived long enough to have additional children.

I'll admit that these viewpoints may be narrow-minded. As we began working through Daniel's challenges, my mindset expanded. Daniel's challenges were taking over our family's time and finances. I was prepared to continue that level of attention and investment to focus on him, to help him as much as possible. That one child became even more precious. My new purpose was helping Daniel.

But also, with my recent miscarriages, I was getting emotionally exhausted from the start/stop distress that miscarriages cause. It is such an emotional roller coaster to wait, start, hope, hope, hope, stop, grieve, wait, start, hope, hope, hope, stop, grieve (no, not again!). I was not sure I could wait and start and hope and grieve anymore. I was reaching a point of emotional exhaustion, yet I didn't even have a late-stage miscarriage, or something else very tragic. I began to understand many more reasons of why couples might just have one child.

As I mentioned, two months after the molar pregnancy ended, Daniel was diagnosed with autism. Some people would kindly suggest that it had been "for the best" that the molar had happened, since it would have been very difficult to have a newborn and work through all the adjustments of now also having an older child with special needs. I can see this point and try to take some comfort in it. Without the second baby in the mix, I was able to fully focus on Daniel and his needs. This is true. However, I have never been thankful for the original miscarriage or the molar pregnancy. I gained wisdom and compassion from them. I am thankful for the wisdom and expanded understanding, but not for the loss of what could have been.

When I meet couples now who have one child, I try to see their situation with more compassion, even if I never get the full story. While they truly and happily may have chosen to have the one child and not try for a second, I now understand that that many of their stories may also be associated with a lot of pain. Their specific story is none of my business unless they want to share it. They do not owe anyone their story. I have learned through our experience that family planning is not always easy and does not go according to plan, for many couples. Ours started out nice and easy with my first pregnancy, but a lot of uncertainty entered in along the way.

I can easily now see how we may have only had one child. I do not take for granted the miracle of life.

- **We Wanted a Sibling for Daniel**

Carrie (Mother): With Daniel as our first and only child, we felt it would be good for him to have a sibling. A younger child would, without question, get in his business and force increased flexibility from Daniel. A younger sibling wouldn't initially know or understand Daniel's challenges and, therefore, would not tiptoe around him. A new child would have expectations of Daniel as a big brother. We felt this would be healthy for our whole family. Additionally, as the second child grew older, we could teach him/her about Daniel's experience. We saw having a second child as the opportunity to create a deeper, richer family experience.

- **The Choice to Play the Odds**

Carrie (Mother): Beyond delaying a new addition to our family, the molar did something else. It absolutely took away our opportunity to have a second child while ignorant (some might say innocent) of already having a child with autism. Now that we had a child diagnosed with autism, there were new viewpoints to consider and battle in our decision to expand our family. People would suggest to us that autism has a genetic component. Would it be "reckless" to purposefully enter into another pregnancy knowing there was a possibility of having another child on the spectrum?

- **We Decided to Try Again**

Carrie (Mother): As we considered a second child in the wake of a couple of miscarriages, we also considered adoption. We decided we would try another round for our own biological child, see how it went, and then possibly consider adoption - possibly the adoption of a child with special needs. As I considered getting pregnant, I did fear that with my age advancing into my later 30s, perhaps I would have a second child with Downs Syndrome...so I would have one with autism and one with Downs Syndrome. This was a fear I had, but I was willing to take the risk; I was willing to face that struggle. Jake and I were prepared and equipped to care for either a second child with autism, or one that might have some other condition.

Caleb was my fourth pregnancy. It went smoothly, just like my pregnancy with Daniel.

- **What Did I Do Differently?**

Carrie (Mother): After Daniel's diagnosis, we saw positive changes in Daniel when we began therapy (behavioral, speech, occupational therapy) and his food diet (gluten free, dairy free). I wondered and regretted that maybe things would have been different for Daniel if I had made different choices related to his environmental influences. I assumed and worried that Caleb, as a young child, would have similar predispositions as Daniel.

Therefore, I took steps to improve the course for my second baby based on what we had learned from Daniel. I changed a few things. I made new choices about the foods I ate while pregnant with Caleb. I altered the way I approached breast feeding in order to increase my milk production. And, when Caleb did begin drinking formula, I selected a hypoallergenic option.

Additionally, while we have no evidence that vaccinations caused or exacerbated Daniel's autism symptoms, Jake and I have adopted a slower pace to receiving vaccinations for Caleb. I am not against vaccines, but we have adjusted our approach. This is not a medical recommendation. This is just what we have done for Caleb.

On this note, I recommend reading literature about vaccines, and you can form your own point of view. I would encourage you to become familiar with terms such as "essential", "cost-effective", "efficacy", "transmission", and "risk of exposure" (Vaccine Information Statements, 2017; Eisenstein, 2010). Each vaccine has information related to these terms. I would also recommend researching why certain vaccines are offered at particular ages. You can then draw your own conclusions about how you plan immunizations for your child.

- **A Father Again, to Caleb**

Jacob (Father): Most recently (which has completely opened my eyes to what we truly missed with Daniel in terms of the "typical" progression of growth and development), I've been watching our second son, Caleb. Watching Caleb sparks a sense of joy in my heart from knowing that he has not had the same struggles and difficulties as Daniel, which then produces heartache surrounding the memories we should have had with Daniel which we are now only experiencing with Caleb. In the simplest of terms, it is night and day. None of this is to say that we don't have absolutely wonderful memories of experiences with Daniel, but as monumental as most of those memories were (and are) in our minds, all the things that Caleb is doing naturally is light years ahead of where Daniel was at age 2½ years old. And since we didn't experience the same things with Daniel as we did with Caleb at such a young age, we are literally astonished on a weekly basis about what we see Caleb doing naturally, knowing now that we missed those things with Daniel.

Here is the thing that I understand about the situation of childhood development: all kids develop and grow at different rates, and skills emerge at different times. In our family and with our boys, we were absolutely amazed at how naturally and easily the same skills came to our non ASD child; skills which took so long to develop for our ASD child. I do not think that I can state with enough emphasis how amazing it is to see a child's typical development. It is beautiful to see. It has almost seemed like a constant course of miracles happening every single day.

Chapter Summary:

- Once we had a child diagnosed with autism, there were new points of view to consider and battle in our decision to expand our family.
- Jake and I felt prepared and equipped to care for either a second child with autism, or one that might have some other condition.
- Having a first child struggling to achieve so many early developmental milestones has given us an immeasurable appreciation for all the milestones our second "typical" child achieves without early intervention. We feel blessed to have both experiences.

Afterword

Carrie (Mother): Thank you so much for spending time learning about my journey with Daniel. It is a journey that continues, and I am still learning how to best support him as he faces new successes and new challenges. I have found great support and blessing and understanding through my experience as Daniel's mother. I am his only mother, and I want to be a good one to him. I know that you must feel the same way about your role as a parent to your child and children.

A frustration and saddening reality of mine early on was that I was functioning in a world where one out of every forty-two boys is diagnosed with autism (Autism Prevalence, 2017). Yet, I didn't see those children anywhere. Where are all the impacted children? Where are their parents? I was there, moving around in the world, but I could not identify many other people like me. This was enlightening to me because I had never really wondered this before. Where are all the children with special needs? There are so many of them, not just with autism but with other special needs and disabilities. They are mostly invisible to most people, unless you work in the industry or have a child with special needs.

As a parent of a child with special needs, I've realized it is easier to keep your child at home than to take him with you to the grocery store. It's easier to not go to church than to leave your biting child in the nursery where he might harm another child. Or, simply because they have so many special needs, you cannot leave them with someone untrained, or someone who doesn't understand their food sensitivities or their medication schedule. What do you do with a non-verbal child? How do you trust someone else to care for them? And how much does that type of good care cost? Or, if you are able to go out with your child, who wants all the looks from other "typical" people if your child is stimming, saying weird things, being too loud, or having a meltdown?

Because of some of Daniel's difficulties, I often gave up and just wanted to keep him home. It's easier and less expensive to just stay home, but that then means you are staying out of the world, not interacting, and are becoming more closed off and feeling more isolated. How many parents feel this way? You are in homes, in therapy sessions, in hospitals and clinics, and in special schools. You rely on delivery services, you read books, you watch television, and you try to get some rest when you can. You are not in the mall, not at the movies, not in public schools, not in parks, not in the library, not in church, not at concerts, not in restaurants, and not on vacation.

One reason I'm writing this book is to acknowledge all of the parents who are struggling in the world, but who feel separated from it. I hope this book can give you some encouragement to know that you are not forgotten not by me. I wish I knew who you and your children are.

- **My New Normal**

Jacob (Father): One moment when I pretty much realized that my life with my son was going to be as close to "normal" as normal can get was when I first let go of his bike seat and he just started pedaling as if it came naturally. He rode his bike for the first time that day, without training wheels. My face hurt for three days because of how much I was smiling as I chased him all over the park. I must have run alongside of him for 20 minutes, to be there if he fell or was about to crash.

As the father of a son with special needs, I had let go of some of the activities I wanted for him. But in the process, I may have limited my expectation of what he could do by not expecting him to do things as quickly as typical kids. When he rode his bike for the first time without training wheels, it was a huge moment for me because it deeply convinced me not to put restraints on him for accomplishing whatever he wants to do, but to encourage him all the more in trying harder to push his limits in whatever activity he was doing. When it came to riding his bike, he was right on par with, if not ahead of, many kids his age. In this moment of bliss, I just let him ride...my new normal!

Carrie and Jacob (Parents): We are able to more fully appreciate and enjoy the miracles of our children because of our journey with Daniel. Parts of the journey we would not have asked for, but we now cherish every step.

References: Books, Printed Materials, and Websites

1. American Psychiatric Association (2000). Diagnostic and Statistical Manual of Mental Disorders (4th ed.), Text Revision, Washington, DC, American Psychiatric Association.

2. American Psychiatric Association (2013). Diagnostic and Statistical Manual of Mental Disorders (5TH ed.), Washington, DC, American Psychiatric Association.

3. Autism's Associated Medical and Mental-Health Conditions (2017). Retrieved from www.autismspeaks.com.

4. Autism Prevalence. (2017). Retrieved from www.autismspeaks.com.

5. Baker, B. L. & Brightman, A. J. (2004). Steps to Independence: Teaching Everyday Skills to Children With Special Needs. Brookes Publishing; 4th edition.

6. Brown, R. (1973). A First Language: The Early Stages. Cambridge, MA: Harvard University Press.

7. Center for Disease Control. (2017). Community Report on Autism 2016. https://www.cdc.gov/ncbddd/autism/documents/community_report_autism.pdf

8. Center for Disease Control. (2017). Developmental Milestones, tracking resources website: http://www.cdc.gov/ncbddd/actearly/index.html

9. Center for Disease Control. (2017). General Recommendations on Immunization. Retrieved from https://www.cdc.gov/vaccines/pubs/pinkbook/downloads/genrec.pdf.

10. Center for Disease Control. (2017). Screening and Diagnosis for Healthcare Providers. Retrieved from http://www.cdc.gov/ncbddd/autism/hcp-screening.html.

11. Center for Disease Control. (2017). Vaccine Information Statements (VIS). Retrieved from https://www.cdc.gov/vaccines/hcp/vis/current-vis.html.

12. Center for Parent Information and Resources. (2017). 10 Basic Steps of Special Education, Newark, NJ, No author. Retrieved from http://www.parentcenterhub.org/steps/.

13. Cooper, J. O., Heron, T. E., & Heward, W. L. (2007) Applied Behavior Analysis. Pearson; 2 edition.

14. DSM-5™ Diagnostic Criteria (2017). Retrieved from www.autismspeaks.com.

15. Edelson, S. M., & Rimland, B. (2006). Recovering Autistic Children. San Diego, CA. Autism Research Institute.

16. Eisenstein, M. (2010). Make an Informed Vaccine Decision for the Health of Your Child. Santa Fe, NM. New Atlantean Press.

17. Garland, T. (2014). Self-Regulation Interventions and Strategies: Keeping the Body, Mind & Emotions on Task in Children with Autism, ADHD or Sensory Disorders._PESI Publishing & Media.

18. Gates, D. (2017) The Body Ecology Diet & Autism. Retrieved from https://s3-us-west 2.amazonaws.com/beautism/bedrobroch0609st.pdf

19. Gottschall, E. (2010). Breaking the Vicious Cycle, Intestinal Health Through Diet. Ontario, Canada. Kirkton Press Ltd.

20. HLA-DQB1 Gene. (2017). Genetics Home Reference. Retrieved from https://ghr.nlm.nih.gov/gene/HLA-DQB1#conditions.

21. Kubler-Ross, E. & Kessler, D. (2014) On Grief and Grieving: Finding the Meaning of Grief Through the Five Stages of Loss. Scribner; Reprint edition.

22. Lipkin, P. H., Okamoto, J. (2015). The Individuals With Disabilities Education Act (IDEA) for Children With Special Educational Needs. American Academy of Pediatrics. 136(6).

23. McCandless, J., (2009). Children with Starving Brains, A Medical Treatment Guide for Autism Spectrum Disorder. Bramble Books, 4th Edition.

24. Melillo, R. (2010). Disconnected Kids. New York, NY. Penguin Group.

25. Minshawi, N. F., Hurwitz, S., Fodstad, J. C., Biebl, S., & McDougle, C. J. (2014) The Association Between Self-Injurious Behaviors and Autism Spectrum Disorders. Psychology Research and Behavior Management, (7) 125-136.

26. Rogers, S. J., & Dawson, G. (2009) Early Start Denver Model for Young Children with Autism: Promoting Language, Learning and Engagement. The Guilford Press; 1 edition.

27. Serrousi, K., and Rimland, B. (2002). Unraveling the Mystery of Autism and Pervasive Developmental Disorder: A Mother's Story of Research & Recovery. New York, NY. Simon & Schuster.

Notes

Notes

Notes

About the Authors

Casi Olson, M.A. in Clinical Psychology, LMHC/LPC

Casi is a Licensed Mental Health Counselor (LMHC), with her Master's Degree in Clinical Psychology. Casi possesses an intense desire to help families and children. She has a specific focus on autism-related behaviors and challenges. Casi delivers a tailored and family-centered approach, which she promotes through her private practice, ETS Therapy Services. ETS stands for Empower, Teach, and Support. Casi does exactly those things for her families and clients, in that order. Whether her clients are 2 or 42, Casi will empower, teach, and support them.

In her practice, Casi draws from principles of Applied Behavior Analysis (ABA), Behavior Therapy, and Humanistic Psychology. Before opening her practice, Casi worked for the University of Washington Autism Center as a Behavior and Education Consultant, where she managed ABA therapy programs, trained agencies, and consulted school districts throughout the state of Washington.

Casi earned her B.A. in Psychology from the University of Puget Sound and her M.A. in Clinical Psychology at Argosy University (Seattle). As part of her training, she joined highly respected programs in autism research and ABA therapy. She participated as a therapist in the Early STAART Denver Model project and the Early STEPS Study. These projects were randomized clinical trials of intensive early intervention for toddlers with autism. Casi also has deep experience in the methods of both Discrete Trial Training, and the ABA Pivotal Response Training technique.

Carrie Woolman, Mother of a child diagnosed with autism

Carrie is married to Jacob Woolman, and they have 2 boys. Their older boy, Daniel, was diagnosed with autism at age 2 ½. Carrie and Jake were stunned by how much there was to learn about autism and Daniel's needs. They dove into the learning process with a high level of energy and determination to help Daniel reach his full potential, without knowing what his full potential would be. Carrie and Jake want to share their experience and knowledge with other parents who may now be facing a diagnosis, so that the uncertain next steps might be easier to find, and take.

Originally from Texas, Carrie has lived in Washington State since completing her undergraduate studies at Duke University. She also earned a Master's in Business Administration from the University of Washington. Carrie works as a marketing professional. Jacob is a stay-at-home dad, having previously worked for several years in the construction industry. He earned his undergraduate degree from Northwest University in Washington.

54781139R00115

Made in the USA
San Bernardino, CA
23 October 2017